Praise for *Finance Secrets of Billion-Dollar Entrepreneurs*

"Dileep's research supports the failure of our venture capital system and the success of 'bootstrapping'! His work reaffirms that the skills needed to be successful as an entrepreneur are learned, and when acted upon, produce real results in starting a successful business."

—**Ed Flaherty,** Founder of Rapid Oil Change

"With the voice of an entrepreneur, the insight of a scholar and the wisdom of experience, Rao provides a clear road map for how entrepreneurs can grow successful companies while maintaining control of their ventures!"

—**Dr. Raymond Smilor**, Emeritus Professor of Entrepreneurship, Neeley School of Business, TCU

"Dileep Rao's *Finance Secrets of Billion-Dollar Entrepreneurs* provides entrepreneurs practical guidance on how to scale their business via finance-smart strategies without giving up unnecessary control. I'd consider this a must-read for anyone with entrepreneurial spirit looking to establish a successful, long-term enterprise!"

—**Phil Krump,** Head of Strategic Growth & Operations | Expansion Markets, BMO Harris Bank

"A good idea with a finance-smart plan is invaluable...that's what makes Dr. Rao's book invaluable."

—**Dr. Stephen T. Barnett**, Fulbright Specialist, SCORE Mentor, Visiting Professor, Management Center Innsbruck, Austria, and Marketing Professor Emeritus, Stetson University

"*Finance Secrets of Billion-Dollar Entrepreneurs* helps entrepreneurs develop a road map to their start-up dreams. This book shows them how America's billion-dollar entrepreneurs created wealth and kept more of it—without losing it all to investors and VCs, and how you can, too. Having financed more than four hundred businesses and real-estate projects and managed five turnaround ventures, Dileep Rao knows venture financing and venture turnarounds first-hand. To write this book, he interviewed and analyzed eighty-seven-billion-dollar entrepreneurs who built their businesses from start-up to more than one billion dollars in sales and valuation (and interviewed twenty-three hundred-million-dollar entrepreneurs). His findings are documented in this book. Read it to learn how to take off without venture capital."

—**William Rudelius,** University of Minnesota marketing professor and coauthor of twenty-four editions of business textbooks

"This book delivers clear thinking for entrepreneurs who want to control their own destiny and grow their business without the need for venture capital."

—**Joel Cannon,** cofounder and president of Cannon Technologies and serial technology company entrepreneur

"Succeeding as an entrepreneur requires capital-efficient, not capital-intensive, financial management. Among the 'secrets' Rao unveils: Founders rarely benefit by acquiring venture capital early in the lifecycle of their start-up. *Finance Secrets of Billion-Dollar Entrepreneurs* is a how-to guide for finance-smart innovators, replete with examples from Amazon to Zara."

—**Tariq Samad,** Sr. Fellow, Technological Leadership Institute, University of Minnesota

"In his new book, *Finance Secrets of Billion-Dollar Entrepreneurs*, Dileep Rao breaks an age-old myth that "in order to be really successful, entrepreneurs need venture capital." He not only dispels the myth but demonstrates how entrepreneurs can be even more successful by not going down the VC path. Dileep's book is must-read material for every business owner looking to build their empire."

—**Brian Moran,** CEO, Small Business Edge

"Rao writes for the entrepreneur for whom extreme wealth and extreme control of his or her business are of equal importance. Rao's genius is in his rock-solid understanding of the kind of thinking needed, the kinds of choices that need to be made and the tactics that make it possible to go big but to go it on your own. His approach isn't easy, but his writing makes it all clear and with that clarity provides the path to possibility for the entrepreneur who reads this book."

—**Jerome Katz,** Brockhaus Chair in Entrepreneurship, Chaifetz School of Business, Saint Louis University

"[Fastenal] grew with the skills and strategies noted in this book. Dr. Rao has done a wonderful job of analyzing my experience and that of many other unicorn-entrepreneurs in the US. And he has put together a book that everyone should read if they want to know how to build a growth venture, even a billion-dollar venture, and do it with internal cash flow and capital they control. I know the world has changed since I started Fastenal and that there are more venture capitalists today. But as this book shows, very few entrepreneurs get venture capital, and even fewer succeed with it or gain from it. Your best option is to get the skills and use the smart strategies noted by Dr. Rao in this book. Good luck."

—**Bob Kierlin,** cofounder of Fastenal

FINANCE

SECRETS

OF BILLION-DOLLAR
ENTREPRENEURS

FINANCE

SECRETS

OF BILLION-DOLLAR
ENTREPRENEURS

Venture Finance without
Venture Capital

Dileep Rao

**Business
Press**

Coral Gables

SECRETS

Table of Contents

Foreword

This isn't just another book on entrepreneurship. If you are reading this, chances are you are looking for a how-to on financing your dream enterprise OR you are a successful entrepreneur looking for the right way to grow your venture. Not only does Dileep Rao give entrepreneurs a clear and no-nonsense road map to financing ventures in *Finance Secrets of Billion-Dollar Entrepreneurs*, but he does so while asking you to look beyond conventional wisdom, using methods aimed at keeping you in the driver's seat.

The road to the pinnacle of entrepreneurship can seem like a steep climb. While it does take a lot of hard work to carry your venture from concept to thriving reality, the wrong decisions in key moments—especially when you are looking to grow and expand—can result in all your hard work going down the drain. This book's key message of delaying or completely avoiding external financing (VC)—not only to successfully fund and grow your business, but to do so while staying in control—is one of many smart strategies outlined and explained in detail by Dileep in *Finance Secrets* that resonates with me.

The road to becoming CEO of a successful multi-million-dollar company started in college. In 2004, with just $375 and a need to pay my out-of-state tuition, I built a merchandise liquidation company. Eventually, I was working with huge companies like Macy's and CVS. My business grew with internal financing, and, when I saw the opportunity in the subscription beauty-box business in 2013, I took it. I was able to count on my previous growth to start BoxyCharm. I was not interested in copying what others were doing. As Dileep points out in his study of successful entrepreneurs like Steve Jobs and Bill Gates, among others, I knew the key to capitalizing on an emerging trend was to stand out by improving what was being offered to the consumer.

My success, and the success of other unicorn-entrepreneurs discussed in this book, is proof that you don't need venture capital to start your business or to fuel your growth. And you certainly don't need to give away ownership and control of your dream in exchange for financing. Don't take my word for it. Just look at the author's own track record. Entrepreneurs and leaders from around the world—including Fortune 500 companies—count on Dileep's advice in venture financing and business development. Trust me, wherever you are in your journey as an entrepreneur, you'll learn a great deal.

Yosef Martin
Founder and CEO of BoxyCharm

Introduction

There is not enough venture capital (VC) to satisfy the world's entrepreneurial dreams. Even with VC, more ventures fail than succeed. But all entrepreneurs can benefit by getting the expertise to take off without VC—and then decide whether or not to use it. With shows like *Shark Tank* and the constant publicity drumbeat from Silicon Valley, nearly all entrepreneurs have been deceived into thinking that they need angel capital and VC to build a giant venture. But this is not true. I wrote this book to show you the reality from the entrepreneur's perspective—how more than 90 percent of America's billion-dollar entrepreneurs finance their ventures and take off without VC and nearly 80 percent never use it.

Can you create a billion-dollar business without taking a penny of VC? 76 percent of America's unicorn-entrepreneurs do just that; and 18 percent receive VC after they have already built their venture and proven their leadership potential—allowing the entrepreneurs to control the venture capitalists instead of the other way around.

If you are the owner of one of the millions of businesses succeeding every day without VC, this book will teach you how to dominate your industry and scale your business without losing control of the venture.

Two key questions are: Can you avoid VC? Or can you delay VC till take off and still succeed?

A prevailing and quite popular belief is that entrepreneurs need VC to grow. With twenty-three years as a financier (in equity, debt, and leases), including success managing five turnarounds, I, too, at one time believed in the importance of financiers.

But when I interviewed seven billion-dollar entrepreneurs and twenty-three one-hundred-million-dollar entrepreneurs[1] and analyzed the strategies of eighty billion-dollar entrepreneurs,[i] my thinking shifted. I found that more than ninety percent of America's billion-dollar entrepreneurs in the VC era (since 1946) had avoided or delayed VC. In Silicon Valley, most delayed VC. Outside Silicon Valley, most completely avoided it.

They used finance-smart expertise to link their business and finance strategies to grow more with less, to finance for control, and to launch before the end of the runway. This book offers their proven strategies that help to link business and finance, to grow without VC or with delayed VC, and to control the venture and wealth created.

Need for Finance-Smart Expertise

As you will see, finance-smart expertise helps entrepreneurs grow and maintain control of their enterprise.

VCs fund very few ventures. About 99.9 percent of ventures will not get VC, and 80 percent of those who do get it fail. This means that only about 0.02 percent of ventures gain after obtaining VC. Even among the 0.02 percent who benefit from VC, finance-smart entrepreneurs retain control of their venture and do better than the others.

VC works in a few select industries and areas. VC-funded home runs have mostly dominated emerging industries, and they have done well mainly in Silicon Valley. In contrast, finance-smart entrepreneurship works for all, everywhere and at any stage.

---

i   Billion-dollar entrepreneurs are defined as those who start (or co-start) their business and are involved in its growth until it reaches $1 billion in sales and valuation

VCs mainly finance after they have seen evidence of potential. Finance-smart expertise helps entrepreneurs develop ventures both before and after there is evidence of potential. After this potential is evident, some entrepreneurs seek VC. Most do not.

Among America's billion-dollar entrepreneurs, those who were finance smart and avoided VC kept the highest proportion of the wealth they created followed closely by those who delayed VC. Those who were the least finance smart and got VC early and were replaced as CEOs kept the smallest proportion. As an example, Steve Jobs got VC early and kept a very small proportion of the wealth he created in Apple. Jeff Bezos delayed VC and kept a much higher proportion of the wealth created by Amazon.com. Michael Bloomberg avoided VC and kept more than 80 percent of the wealth created in his company.

Capital-intensive, VC-seeking ventures need money constantly. Entrepreneurs who use the capital-intensive strategy continuously need cash for their venture because they spend faster than their influx of cash, and because of poor forecasts. There are too many unknowns in new ventures and emerging industries to forecast accurately. This constant search for the next round of funding can feel like a runway that needs extending while the plane is in motion.

Additionally, emerging industries don't take off immediately. Many entrepreneurs expect a fast takeoff with limited cash, especially when a new industry emerges. When reality turns out to be worse than expectations, ventures run out of cash. A cash-guzzling venture can fail if it cannot raise additional capital or cannot switch to capital efficiency quickly.

Entrepreneurs who raise a limited amount of cash may not be able to get more. Billion-dollar entrepreneurs are able to grow with limited cash by being finance smart.

Finance-Smart Expertise Links Business and Finance

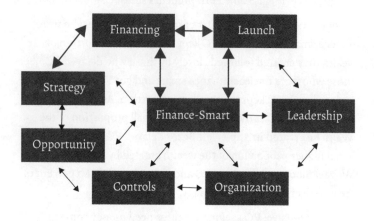

Figure 1. The Finance-Smart Business

Finance-smart strategies used by billion-dollar entrepreneurs combine business-smart, capital-smart, and leadership-smart skills and strategies:

- 💰 Business-smart
  - ‣ Opportunity: What you sell?
  - ‣ Strategy: How to dominate?
- 💰 Capital-smart
  - ‣ Financing: How to fund needs with control?
  - ‣ Launch: How to take off with limited cash?
- 💰 Leadership-smart
  - ‣ Controls: How to control as the business grows?
  - ‣ Organize: Developing an effective corporation?
  - ‣ Leadership: How to become a dominating leader?

Finance-smart entrepreneurs plan and act holistically. They don't develop their opportunity and strategy in a vacuum and then seek financing. They understand finance and its impacts. They design, adjust, and link the business based on the financial implications in order to grow with capital efficiency.

Business-Smart Skills & Strategies

Business-smart strategies include finding the opportunity and developing the strategy to create more wealth per dollar of capital used. This means finding and proving growth strategies with minimal investment and growing with limited resources.

OPPORTUNITY STRATEGIES FOR MORE POTENTIAL PER DOLLAR: Finding the right opportunity for high growth without capital is not easy because you need to use your skills and passion to develop a competitive advantage in a high-potential trend. Passion helps entrepreneurs become better than competitors, even with fewer resources. Trends spur growth as customers migrate more easily toward the emerging industry. Without an expanding industry, you need to capture market share to grow. But grabbing market share is difficult to do without a competitive advantage. Entrepreneurs often seek increased share by starting a price war, but this is dangerous for a new venture with limited resourcesunless you have an edge that your competitors cannot imitate.

When Jeff Bezos was starting Amazon.com, he was able to seek higher market shares by competing with a lower price against the established giants, Borders and Barnes & Noble. But he succeeded because his costs were significantly lower since he used the Internet to avoid the fixed and variable costs of stores.

BUSINESS STRATEGIES FOR MORE EDGE PER DOLLAR:
Your finance-smart business strategy should include the right combination of product, customers, and advantage. The business strategy affects your advantage, growth, pricing, and potential. Often, the business strategy can be more important than your product, especially if your product can be easily imitated. Since the first strategy may not be right, billion-dollar entrepreneurs often pivoted to get an edge. This group includes Sam Walton (Walmart), Bill Gates (Microsoft), and Travis Kalanick (Uber). As examples, Sam Walton shifted from owning small Ben Franklin stores to starting the big-box Walmart store when big boxes emerged. Bill Gates changed from writing software to licensing an operating system. Travis Kalanick shifted from renting limos to developing the cab-without-cab model. Bootstrap and test your strategy.

Capital-Smart Skills & Strategies

Capital-smart strategies include using the right financial structure that is linked to the opportunity and to the business strategy; finding the right balance of internal and external financing; using the right sources, instruments, amounts, and uses by stage; and knowing how to control cash flow in real time to get more controllable capital. By cutting risk, keeping control, and taking off with limited capital, entrepreneurs enhance value and reduce dilution.

FINANCING STRATEGIES FOR MORE GROWTH PER DOLLAR:
Most billion-dollar entrepreneurs did not get VC at all or did not get VC until they started growing. After their venture started growing and their potential was evident, either they grew without capital, or attracted VC without losing control. Jan Koum (WhatsApp) grew with financing from his partner and angels. By

the time he attracted VC, he was able to control the venture. What this means is that you need to be able to take off with the limited capital available from alternate financing sources.

LAUNCH STRATEGIES FOR MORE TAKEOFF PER DOLLAR:
The capital-intensive growth strategy requires lots of cash. The capital-smart method is to launch with limited cash and make sure you never run out. This means using the right timing and growth rate; finding the right resources, developing the right sales, marketing, and operations strategies; and reducing finance needs till takeoff. Dick Schulze of Best Buy was able to grow by building big stores when they emerged. He had an unfair edge over his small-business competitors, used trade credit to finance his inventory, used leases, and focused on sales to fund the business.

Leader-Smart Skills & Strategies

Leader-smart strategies include designing the right controls, developing an effective organization, and leading as CEO to dominate your industry. Entrepreneurs who seek VC after evidence of venture potential, but before evidence of leadership are replaced by a professional CEO. To stay on as CEO, you need a track record in a previous venture or you need to prove it, with performance, in the current one.

This Book

This book focuses on the skills and strategies of finance-smart entrepreneurs. It gives you the steps to follow and helps you understand that the reality of America's most successful entrepreneurs is not the rarified fantasy of *Shark Tank*, which most perceive to be the world of venture capital.

Billion-dollar entrepreneurs attain the skills to find the right opportunity and competitive edge to grow in a hot emerging industry or trend and the skills to launch the venture with limited resources.

They use the right internal and external financing strategy to launch their venture and capture potential. After Aha, when their potential is evident, they use customized capital strategies to take off and dominate.

Along with the right financing, they use customized launch strategies to dominate their industry with less capital. To do this, they grow at the right pace and focus for the right edge. If their first choice is not right, they pivot.

With these skills and strategies, they grow, dominate, control, and succeed. That's what this book covers.

Part I

Pre-Finance: Link Business & Finance

There are two ways to build giant ventures. The first is the capital-intensive, venture capital method. The second is the capital-efficient, billion-dollar-entrepreneur method. 99.98 percent of entrepreneurs will not benefit from the capital-intensive method because they will not get VC, not want VC, or not succeed with VC, and can benefit from the capital-efficient method. The remaining 0.02 percent will benefit from the capital-efficient method by delaying VC and keeping control of the venture and the wealth created. To take off without VC, entrepreneurs need to link business and finance.

To take-off without VC, entrepreneurs need to know how to take-off with less. To take-off with less, entrepreneurs need to know how finance affects every part of their venture and adjust their business.

This chapter shows how billion-dollar entrepreneurs link their business and finance strategies to grow with control.

What Venture Capitalists Do

Venture capitalists are private equity investors that provide funds to startups that exhibit high growth potential, and they do so in exchange for equity in the company.

Venture capitalists (VCs) wait for Aha, when the venture's potential is evident. There are too many ventures seeking VC. According to VC lore, they reject about 99 out of 100 ventures that seek their capital. So, they need to see proof of potential, i.e. Aha, before they invest in a venture.

There are basically four types of Aha:

- 💰 **PREVIOUS-UNICORN AHA:** If Elon Musk wants to raise VC for a new venture, he will have VCs lined up outside his door. VCs are more likely to offer financing to entrepreneurs who have already built one unicorn under the assumption that these entrepreneurs have the skills to build another. The rest of us who have not developed unicorns need to prove our potential with one of the other Aha's.

- 💰 **OPPORTUNITY AHA:** If VCs see a billion-dollar technology and the potential is evident, they may fund it. Herb Boyer, one of the team that split the gene, had no trouble getting VC for his venture Genentech. There are not many such billion-dollar entrepreneurs who got VC after developing their opportunity. Steve Jobs, one of the greatest entrepreneurs of the last fifty years, was funded by angels. An angel investor, or private investor, is an individual with high net worth who provides capital for an early-stage startup, often in exchange for ownership equity. More than ten VCs rejected him before they could see potential in his strategy.

💰 **STRATEGY AHA:** Steve Jobs got VC after his growth strategy was evident. So did Pierre Omidyar of eBay. These entrepreneurs have to launch their ventures with their own savings, and money from family and angels, i.e. with limited capital. After their strategy is evident, they get VC and are replaced as CEO by professionals.

💰 **BILLION-DOLLAR-LEADERSHIP AHA:** Most billion-dollar entrepreneurs receive VC after their venture's potential and their leadership skills are evident. Most of the billion-dollar-entrepreneurs who get VC fall into this category. They develop the skills to take-off without VC. Facebook's Mark Zuckerberg fits in this category.

What Finance-Smart Entrepreneurs Do

Finance-smart entrepreneurs take off without VC and get to Aha. After reaching Aha, when their potential is evident to themselves and to the world, they have options. They can seek VC or avoid it. About 24 percent of billion-dollar entrepreneurs get VC after reaching Aha. The remaining 76 percent continue growing without VC.

To take off without VC, they reach Aha with the optimum combination of internal financing and external financing that does not seek control. After reaching Aha, they get growth financing from late-stage VC, public markets, or internal financing to continue growing.

This chapter shows how finance-smart billion-dollar entrepreneurs take off without VC by linking their business and finance strategies to grow more with less.

Chapter 1

Select the Right Growth Track

Billion-dollar entrepreneurs use skills and strategies to link business and finance. By linking these two things, they reduce or postpone financial needs until attaining money becomes cheaper and non-controlling. In the long run, linking does not weaken their business. Instead, linking makes the business stronger.

Many entrepreneurs write their business plan for their start-up or growing venture and immediately seek equity or VC financing. The reality is that about 99.99 percent of ventures are unlikely to get VC. Those who do receive VC do so after there is evidence of their potential to dominate high-growth, emerging industries.

Getting VC financing very early can be a double-edged sword. VC is very expensive in terms of equity dilution, and you will also lose control to the VCs and to a VC-selected CEO. To add injury to insult, about 80 percent of VC-funded ventures fail.

The 20 percent of VC-funded ventures that succeed do so mainly when high-potential industries are emerging, and primarily in Silicon Valley. In Silicon Valley, about 90 percent of billion-dollar entrepreneurs succeed with VC, but most of them delay obtaining VC in order to control their venture and the wealth created. Outside Silicon Valley, more than 90 percent of billion-dollar entrepreneurs avoid VC and stay in control.

This means that more than 99.98 percent of ventures will not get VC or will fail with it. In general, businesses can do better by growing without VC. The remaining 0.02 percent of entrepreneurs can control their ventures and the wealth created by delaying VC.

All entrepreneurs benefit from taking off without VC. After takeoff, you can decide whether to get VC later on. To take off without VC, you need the right skills and the right finance-smart strategies.

This study of America's billion-dollar entrepreneurs suggests the following key lessons for entrepreneurs:

- 💰 You will not get VC before evidence of potential. More than 96 percent of VC is provided after you show proof of your potential to dominate in emerging industries. Entrepreneurs need to take off with a capital-efficient strategy.

- 💰 VCs generally succeed when high-potential industries are emerging. At other times, their track record is not exemplary.

- 💰 VC works in Silicon Valley, but it has not done as well elsewhere. (This topic alone could fill a whole other book.) In fact, most years, the top twenty VCs have been located there, and that is because billion-dollar entrepreneurs in Silicon Valley have mainly used VC, but delayed it till after leadership Aha, when they could stay in control of the venture (more about this later). Interestingly, some of the billion-dollar entrepreneurs outside Silicon Valley such as

Jeff Bezos used Silicon Valley VCs, suggesting that Silicon Valley VCs may have more capital and expertise to win in hotly contested emerging industries. Outside Silicon Valley, more than 90 percent avoided VC. There are many reasons for this phenomenon:

- Billion-dollar entrepreneurs outside Silicon Valley often are in industries that are not of interest to VCs, such as Sara Blakely (Spanx founder) or Thai Lee (CEO of IT provider SHI International)

- Or they are in geographic areas that are not of interest to Silicon Valley VCs, such as Sam Walton, who was based in rural Arkansas

- Or they did not want to cede control to VCs who may prematurely sell off the venture to a strategic buyer in order to become liquid, especially when the public markets are unattractive

- Or they may lose out to Silicon Valley VC-funded ventures that usually can access more resources, which is key in a capital-intensive strategy. But occasionally finance-smart entrepreneurs without VC, such as Michael Dell, have beaten VC-funded ventures with a combination of skills and smart strategies that are covered in this book

💰 Entrepreneurs who are able to obtain VC are rare. Beyond that, entrepreneurs who benefit from VC are rarer. About 99.98 percent of entrepreneurs will not benefit from VC because 99.9 percent will not get it and 0.08 percent will fail with it. Rather than focusing on capital, finance-smart, billion-dollar entrepreneurs focus on building their business and finance their venture with a combination of internal and external capital. Billion-dollar entrepreneurs such as Dick Schulze of Best Buy, Bob Kierlin of Fastenal,

Bill Gates of Microsoft, and Niraj Shah of Wayfair, knew how to get profitable sales with limited capital. And they knew how to develop their business strategy to reduce external needs and increase internal capital. By doing so, they built iconic businesses.

To succeed as an entrepreneur, you need to dominate your market and industry as was done by the finance-smart entrepreneurs who built billion-dollar companies. To dominate and control the wealth you create, it helps to avoid VC or delay VC. To avoid VC or delay VC, it helps to have the right skills to build your business with a combination of sales, internal capital, and external (easily available) capital. That's what we will discuss in this book.

The Right Skills

Most billion-dollar entrepreneurs used the right skills to position *or reposition* their business in order to dominate their emerging industry or emerging trend, and then use the right strategies to lead the business to dominate their industry. The right positioning helps you grow with reduced finance needs and helps you find the right financing to grow with control. Most billion-dollar entrepreneurs do not seek or attract VC until their potential is evident. At that time, most grow without VC, while a few use VC without losing control.

For the right leadership, get the skills to:

- 💰 Select the right growth track
- 💰 Link with the right steps
- 💰 Develop capital-smart skills

The Three Growth Tracks

There are three growth tracks. Two of them allow you to control your venture and the wealth it creates.

To build a giant business from scratch, do you need skills, capital or both? If both, which comes first? Do you need and should you seek VC? When? From whom?

Some common assumptions in venture development today are that entrepreneurs need VC to build a big business; that a business plan helps you get VC; and that VCs are experts at building billion-dollar businesses. Accordingly, many entrepreneurs write a business plan and seek funding from angel investors or VCs. Their hope is to get multiple rounds of VC financing followed by an initial public offering (IPO) and, subsequently, wealth.

Are these assumptions true? Entrepreneurs often assume that they need VC to grow. When you hear about VC home runs, it's usually about how VCs build giants such as Google and Facebook by funding entrepreneurs such as Larry Page, Sergey Brin, and Mark Zuckerberg.

Very few have heard of Vijay Goradia, Thai Lee, Glen Taylor, Bob Kierlin, Jim Leprino, or Richard Burke, all of whom also built giant companies. These entrepreneurs also built giant businesses from scratch, but they did it without VC—and they also made a choice not to focus on seeking publicity. But just because they are not famous does not mean that their strategies cannot help you. They can.

America's most successful entrepreneurs are billion-dollar entrepreneurs who built companies from start-up to more than one billion dollars in sales and valuation. In the last seventy years, since the dawn of the VC age, this group has included entrepreneurs ranging from Sam Walton, Earl Bakken, Bill Gates, and Steve Jobs to Mark Zuckerberg, Steve Ells, Richard Burke, and Kevin Plank.

Billion-dollar entrepreneurs use three growth tracks (Figure 2).

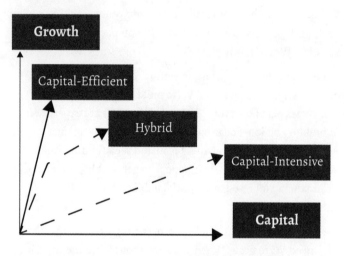

Figure 2. Models to Build Billion-Dollar Companies

CAPITAL-INTENSIVE track, where the entrepreneurs use capital-intensive strategies and obtain VC as soon as possible, i.e. when the opportunity's potential is evident. But since leadership potential has not been proven, these entrepreneurs have to cede control to VCs and leadership to a VC-picked CEO. In this strategy, the venture seeks additional rounds of VC with increasing dilution to entrepreneurs.

Pierre Omidyar used this strategy with eBay. Omidyar started eBay with his personal savings and grew it fast with internal cash flow. But he soon attracted direct competitors with significantly more capital, forcing Omidyar to seek venture capital investment, which recruited a new CEO. Omidyar was significantly diluted by the VCs and the executives. But he did well anyway.

CAPITAL-EFFICIENT track, where the entrepreneurs build their businesses without VC. In this track, entrepreneurs either do not need VC, do not want VC, or cannot get VC. Some in this group get public capital by using an IPO after proving the venture's potential and continue to stay in control. Others stay private. This group includes Dell and Bloomberg.

Michael Dell built his namesake company by knowing how to sell customized personal computers directly from his dorm room. His customers paid when they placed the order. He used that cash, along with terms from his parts vendor, for working capital. The more he sold, the more cash he had, and there was no need for external VC. That is the beauty of the right business model. Michael Bloomberg built his namesake company with alliance capital from Merrill Lynch, who became his first customer. His customers' monthly subscription fees funded his growth.

HYBRID-TRACK, where the entrepreneurs combine both strategies. They are capital efficient before the venture's potential and the entrepreneur's leadership skills are evident, and they're capital intensive afterwards. By delaying VC till their leadership potential is evident, these entrepreneurs stay on as CEOs. They later accept VC and dilution as the price to pay to dominate their emerging industries. By delaying VC and staying on as CEOs, they keep more of the company's wealth than those on the capital-intensive track.

Bill Gates and Mark Zuckerberg followed this strategy. Gates built Microsoft with the fees from licensing the operating system he acquired. He got VC as a way of obtaining an advisor with skin in the game. Mark Zuckerberg built Facebook in his dorm room at Harvard with capital from family and friends. After Facebook took off, he accepted angel capital from Silicon Valley angels, including Peter Thiel. He got VC later. By then, his skills and Facebook's potential were so evident that Zuckerberg obtained proxies to vote the shares of the VCs. That's why he still controls Facebook, even though he does not own a majority of the stock.

Finance-Smart Tracks

Those using the capital-efficient or hybrid growth tracks are termed finance-smart entrepreneurs. Finance-smart entrepreneurship is the expertise to build and control a dominant business by avoiding or delaying VC.

The public image of entrepreneurship has been hijacked by venture capital. The tail is wagging the dog. Unless you have developed a "cure for cancer," you are unlikely to get VC before you have proven your business strategy's potential, and you are unlikely to keep control of your venture until you have proven your leadership potential.

This means you need to know how to get alternate capital to bridge the VC gap and use this limited capital to get to Aha—at which point you may find that you really don't need the dilution or interference of VC.

VC has done well in Silicon Valley, where it has created one of the greatest group of growth companies the world has seen—along with the aura of VC invincibility.

But, have many really gained from VC? And how has VC done outside Silicon Valley? How have billion-dollar entrepreneurs grown outside Silicon Valley?

Let's address these questions.

Chapter 2

Link with the Right Steps

Linking your business and finance strategies helps to make
your business stronger and leaner.

To become capital efficient, link your opportunity, business
strategy and financial strategy. Linking helps you understand
how changes in one area can impact other areas of the business
and how you can adjust to reduce your needs.

Benefits of Linking

Linking can offer fewer surprises, reduced risks, and decreased
losses. Understanding how A affects B, how B influences C, and
how C impacts A does help you, the entrepreneur, to evaluate
what may happen when you make decisions. You start to think
holistically about your entire venture rather than just pieces of it.

This is the expertise that good CEOs have now and all
entrepreneurs need to develop to move forward. Strong CEOs
are trained and tested and have years of experience. Most

importantly, their businesses have histories that help them understand the various relationships in their business and financial models. They can also call upon an experienced team of executives and consultants to help them. Yet many CEOs fail, especially when there is change in the environment caused by new trends, new technologies, and new circumstances.

Entrepreneurs have a tougher job. Their ventures are new, often the trends on which they are being built are new, there are no established markets or vendors, cash flow is usually inadequate, and the venture may not have developed its competitive or management advantage. Entrepreneurs do not have the luxury of learning in a stable corporation as they are climbing the corporate ladder. They have to learn how to build the venture as they are growing it. They have to do it on their own because most ventures have no organization or advisors. And they have to do it with limited resources. This suggests that entrepreneurs need to be able to view the venture as a synergistic whole. They must lead it as a linked organization that makes customers happier to gain an edge and do it with less money because they don't have a choice. So, linking becomes even more important.

Reacting to Inaccurate Sales Projections

The two key unknowns that are inaccurate in the financial projections of a new business are the level of sales, and the needed investment in sales and marketing to generate the sales. Larger and more established companies know—from years of history and their existing relationships with customers and markets—how much they need to spend to generate sales. New businesses have no such luxury. Since sales projections are usually wrong in a start-up, entrepreneurs can gain insight by testing the link between sales and the investment in marketing drivers.

Don Kotula built Northern Tool from a start-up to a unicorn. He started selling log splitters by placing small ads in various magazines that his core market read. These magazines included *Popular Mechanics, Popular Science, Farm World*, and others. He tracked the orders and placed ads only in the magazines that produced results. He also found that there was seasonality to his sales, so he adjusted his marketing accordingly and did not waste money in the low months. He developed his own mailing lists from his ads and got customers' addresses from their checks. He encouraged his customers to refer their friends to receive a catalog, and most of them were happy to do so. This helped Kotula expand his mailing list without a high cost.

Reducing the Need for Early Capital

As mentioned before, early money is expensive money. By linking to make their business capital efficient, most billion-dollar entrepreneurs reduced capital outlay and the need for early VC.

To be capital efficient, it helps to think like VCs. At the beginning of the product-development process, the risk is the highest. You do not know when the product will be ready, what it will look like, what competitors will do, and what the nature of your competitive advantage is. You may have confidence in your abilities, but you could be wrong about the timing and your success in achieving your goals. Also, in emerging industries, timing is another factor since you are not sure when the industry will start to take off. To offset this risk, you need to be confident before investing your cash. If you are frugal and use your resources wisely to make them go the furthest, you could achieve your goals and keep control of the venture and your opportunity.

When he started in 1993, Steve Shank managed Capella University with very few resources. Funding came from his personal assets and from an investment group, and he knew that it would have to last him until accreditation. He spent it only on essentials related to getting accreditation and *took only the risks that he could not avoid*. By 1998, Capella was accredited and could now access federal loans for its students. This enhanced the value of Capella, and it secured funds from NCS in a strategic alliance. Shank knew that desperation is not a good funding strategy. When raising venture capital, the stage of a venture and key milestones (product ready for sale; customers on board; growth; profits) are crucial since they enhance a venture's value. Reach those milestones before you run out of money. As the old saying goes, water is more expensive in the middle of the desert than at either end.

Reducing Cash Needs for Growth

The top skills of billion-dollar entrepreneurs are sales/ marketing and financial management. Using these skills, these entrepreneurs start their businesses with minimal investment. Using nominal levels from external financing sources, they grow by avoiding losses, reducing needs for working capital and fixed assets, and growing with trends.

A business model that needs lots of capital can mean an eventual loss of control to financiers. Designing a business model that grows with little capital and implementing it effectively means that you can grow without capital until the financiers contact you.

Richard Burke founded and built UnitedHealth Group (UNH), a $190 billion+ company. When he first wanted to go public, Burke was told by investment bankers that UNH was not a good candidate for an IPO because it was an "HMO management" company that did not own its health plans. This meant that UNH could book the fees it received for management services and not count the HMO's revenues or profits. Another perceived negative aspect of the company in the minds of investment bankers was that UNH "only" had management contracts—albeit very long and lucrative ones—but not ownership of its HMOs. The bankers' worry was that UNH's HMO customers would cancel the management contracts even though the contracts were long term, even though UNH owned the infrastructure and computer systems of the HMO operations, and the employees of the HMO were on UNH's payroll and under its control. The bankers also overlooked the fact that UNH had no insurance risk, which offset the perceived faults. It could grow faster with less capital and wasn't susceptible to the historical ups and downs of the industry cycle. Eventually, after a successful IPO by a similar firm in Pennsylvania, the investment bankers took UNH public in 1984.

Steps to Link Business and Finance

Many entrepreneurs seek funding by using the "regular" route, i.e. developing a business plan and projections, estimating needs, and making the rounds of investors. This can be frustrating because entrepreneurs without a proven track record are seen as having low credibility.

To improve your projections and, thereby, enhance your credibility, acquire the skills and go backward to link business and finance (Figure 3). Follow these steps:

STEP 1. DEVELOP PROJECTIONS BASED ON YOUR PLAN.
Write your plan and develop financial projections consistent with the plan to gauge your financial needs. As an example, if you plan to use Google to generate sales, develop your projections with numbers showing how much you plan to

spend on Google advertising and the results you expect. Be specific and prove them with actual tests.

STEP 2. TEST YOUR CONCEPT TO REDUCE RISK. Test your opportunity and strategy with real customers without spending too much capital. This will give you real feedback from potential customers and allow you to proceed with more than just guesses. Before selecting Google to generate sales, for example, see what your direct competitors are doing to sell. Then ask your customers to narrow down your options. Test each option till you find the best one. Figure out the results you should expect to avoid wasting money. Bhavin and Divyank Turakhia have built businesses to more than a billion dollars in value. They built their last venture, Media. net, in seven years, from scratch, without venture capital, and sold it for $900 million.[2] They did it by knowing how to avoid paying too much to capture customers.

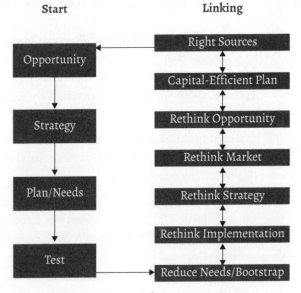

Figure 3. Steps to Link Business & Finance

STEP 3. BOOTSTRAP TO REDUCE NEEDS. Your cost of capital at the start is very high and can range from 80 to 100 percent per year. This means you should postpone what you can and invest only the capital you need to take your business to the next level. Find alternate ways to use the assets you need without investing your cash. For example, lease or rent before you tie your cash in fixed assets.

STEP 4. REEVALUATE YOUR IMPLEMENTATION AND STRATEGIC PLAN TO REDUCE NEEDS. Entrepreneurs make numerous decisions when executing their vision. Can you pick alternative implementation plans that capture your potential while reducing needs? As an example, if your goal is to grow at a very high rate with very high needs, can you reduce your rate slightly without losing your edge, or collect money faster, or focus on customers who pay faster? Can you adjust your strategic plan to reduce your needs while gaining an advantage, or at least not losing your edge? For example, can you sell direct to users rather than selling indirectly via channels? About 75 percent of billion-dollar and hundred-million-dollar entrepreneurs in my study of Minnesota's best entrepreneurs sold direct. With the pervasiveness of the Internet, it is easier to sell direct.

STEP 5. REEXAMINE YOUR MARKET TO REDUCE NEEDS. Your basic business model, what you sell, whom you sell to, and your direct competitors can have a profound impact on your success. As an example, Sam Walton had the same big-box concept and sold the same products as Kmart and Target. But Walton opened his stores in small towns while his competitors focused on the urban market. After he dominated rural America, Walton expanded to urban America and the rest of the world.

STEP 6. RETHINK YOUR OPPORTUNITY FOR MORE ADVANTAGE WITH LOWER NEEDS. Are you selling the right product or service? Are you in sync with the trends? Whole Foods built a giant business by selling organic foods when the trend emerged. Chipotle did the same in quick-serve foods. To build Microsoft, Bill Gates switched from selling the software to selling the operating system.

STEP 7. RE-DO YOUR BUSINESS PLAN WITH CAPITAL EFFICIENCY. Now that you have reconsidered your business based on each step's impact on your capital needs, move forward and rewrite your capital-efficient business plan and projections. Bill Gates started Microsoft with Paul Allen as a company to write software. When Gates found that IBM wanted an operating system for their new line of personal computers, he bought one and licensed it to IBM on a nonexclusive basis. He then rewrote his business plan to license the operating system to nearly all PC manufacturers (except Apple), and then added the Microsoft Office suite of products. He did it all with limited capital and became the richest person in the universe. Gates did get VC, but mainly to get someone with gray hair and a vested interest involved in the company.

STEP 8. RAISE CAPITAL-EFFICIENT NEEDS FROM FINANCE-SMART SOURCES. Find the right sources for your capital-efficient plan, use the best instruments and raise the right amounts by stage so you can grow with control. Mark Zuckerberg is the poster child of this strategy. His first source of funding was friends and family. Next, he got angel capital, followed by VCs. These sources all allowed him to maintain control of the company because they could see how well he was doing at leading the venture and building value. Jan Koum (WhatsApp) did the same.

By going backward to find the best financing for your venture, you are linking your strategy and finance. This makes your business stronger, allows you to grow more with less, and empowers you to control the business and the wealth you create. This is what more than 75 percent of billion-dollar entrepreneurs do in Silicon Valley, and more than 90 percent do outside Silicon Valley.

Chapter 3

Develop Capital-Smart Skills

Billion-dollar entrepreneurs build their venture and control
it with skills before seeking capital.

Capital-smart skills help you link your business to your finance strategies. This helps you better understand the financial impacts of your business strategy and the business impacts of your financial strategy.

Capital-smart skills of billion-dollar entrepreneurs include entrepreneurial accounting skills, controlled financing skills, and capital-efficient launch skills.

Entrepreneurial Accounting Skills

Entrepreneurial accounting is financial management for entrepreneurs. In the Minnesota study, about two-thirds of the billion-dollar and hundred-million-dollar entrepreneurs had expertise in sales/ marketing and financial management. They were "entrepreneurial accountants" who knew how to sell. With skills in financial management and in sales/ marketing, they sold more for less, made more with less, and grew more with less.

Entrepreneurial accounting means knowing your numbers, their impact on your business, and what you can do about them. The following levels of financial expertise help entrepreneurs do more with less.

Level One: Understanding Financial Statements

High-performance entrepreneurs used timely financial data to manage their business. This means getting sales data daily to monitor performance and trends, getting income statements and cash-flow statements weekly (including current assets and current liabilities), and using monthly balance sheets.

When Joel Ronning's first venture to sell Apple products, Mirror Technologies, started to grow, Ronning got financing from angel investors. But he did not develop a good accounting system. Ronning thought he was making money with gross margins of 20 percent to 30 percent, but he was not. His control of accounts receivable was inadequate, and he was not able to turn Mirror around. After leaving Mirror, he spent a "tremendous amount of time" studying finance, accounting, and controls, including items such as contract law, cycle times, receivables, etc. After about two years, Ronning started Tech Squared with $40,000 of financing from credit cards. His first hire was an accountant, and his first capital expenditure was an accounting system. Tech Squared did very well, reaching more than $40 million of sales within four years, and every quarter was profitable. Ronning's third venture, Digital River, reached more than $500 million in revenues.

Level Two: Evaluating Impact of Assumptions

Assumptions can have a key impact on the business. At start-up, all assumptions are unproven. You need to group your assumptions based on their impact and then test the major ones to make sure that the venture has reduced risk and is not wasting resources and time.

The most important assumptions are about sales and the cost to get sales.

Jill Blashack Strahan invested about $20,000 to build Tastefully Simple into a company with sales of more than $100 million. She picked her sales strategy by imitating a proven strategy from another company that was successfully selling through home parties. She tested her concept at annual holiday tours in her hometown. Home parties were ideal venues for tasting, sharing, and having fun. These events were also trend friendly since more women were working outside the home, did not have time to cook elaborate meals, and wanted foods that were simple and affordable. So Blashack Strahan developed the concept of "small indulgences for busy lives." The idea appealed to her because she could sell directly to consumers and it did not require marketing money she did not have or distribution channels she could not access. The home-party strategy was scalable and proven.

Level Three: Analyzing the Financial Impact of the Business Model

Every business model has a financial footprint. The first impact to measure is on your potential sales and cash flow. The second is on the amount of money you need to get sales and cash flow. If neither is attractive, look for alternatives.

For twelve years, Sam Walton tested various business models until the big-box retail store concept took off in urban America.

Uber initially wanted to build a business to rent limos before it switched to its current model. Travis Kalanick found that he could have a bigger impact with the model of peer-based rides.

When Strahan decided to start Tastefully Simple, one of the first things she did after developing a business plan was to run the numbers to see what she could pay her sales consultants. She originally planned to pay out six percent of first-line sales, four percent of second-line sales, and two percent of third-line sales. When she developed her projections with these commissions, Blashack Strahan realized that she would be out of business within four years. So she changed the compensation plan to a 5/3/1 payout.

Level Four: Reducing Financial Needs with Capital Efficiency

Entrepreneurs can reduce their financial needs by knowing how to grow with less. This is more than making small improvements in operations, although that helps. It involves examining the entire venture, the industry, and the trend in order to find the strategy that will enable you to grow more with less.

Bob Kierlin built Fastenal into the country's largest fastener business with an initial investment of $31,000—and no other financing—till he went public. To be able to do this, he built a great service-focused organization and simultaneously reduced needs with capital efficiency. One example of capital efficiency is how Kierlin used space. Initially, Fastenal only had a thousand square feet of space. To take advantage of the lower prices from Japanese manufacturers, Fastenal needed to buy inventory in bulk. This meant that the company needed storage space, and Kierlin started renting nearly all the available residential garage space in Winona, Minnesota on short-term leases. The company kept track of the inventory on three by five index cards. When he opened a new store and needed inventory, Kierlin went to the garages and shipped the inventory to the new store. When he did not need the extra space, he returned control to the homeowner.

Level Five: Finding the Right Financing to Control

One method to fund your business is the capital-intensive VC method. But as noted, about 99.98 percent of entrepreneurs should avoid VC and the rest should delay it. This means that entrepreneurs need to seek alternative methods to finance growth till there is evidence of growth and leadership potential.

Most of the billion-dollar entrepreneurs whose methods I analyzed did just this. About 94 percent of them avoided VC or delayed it. Again, by doing so, they maintained control of their venture and the wealth it created.

Level Six: Real-Time Tracking to Launch with Control

Find out what is important to your business and track it. You don't drive your car without knowing where you are going. Don't run your business without tracking your numbers.

Don Kotula of Northern Tool tracks the sales performance of every store on a daily basis. He compares it to previous periods and to the same day in previous years. He also ranks his stores to track performance, his income statement, inventory, and cash flow, and circulates this information among key decision makers to keep everyone informed about how the company is doing.

Controlled Financing Skills

Financing skills can be a strategic weapon. They can make you more competitive, help you obtain more controllable resources, and reduce unwanted surprises.

Billion-dollar and hundred-million-dollar entrepreneurs are experts at sales and financial management. They have the expertise of both the CEO and CFO, and they know how to get entrepreneurial financing.

Corporate, VC, and Entrepreneurial Financing

While it is easy to assume that all financing is the same, there are major differences between corporate, VC, and billion-dollar entrepreneurial financing.

CORPORATE FINANCING: Corporations have money, but don't like to fund high-risk, unproven ventures in emerging industries. Corporations prefer to finance expansions, and they reduce risk by seeking proven opportunities, funding evolutionary expansions, or acquiring existing businesses.

VC FINANCING: VCs have strict criteria and finance only about 0.1 percent of US ventures. They seek high returns (between 30 percent to 100 percent per year) from ventures that they think will dominate high-potential emerging industries. VCs seek to control the direction and the leadership and seek ventures with the potential to offer high returns in three to five years from an IPO or from a strategic sale.

BILLION-DOLLAR-ENTREPRENEURIAL FINANCING: More than 90 percent of billion-dollar entrepreneurs either avoid or delay VC till they have proven their leadership capacity. Till then, they reduce needs, maximize cash flow, and look for sources that do not seek control. To do this, they use the following five primary skills.

Skills to Avoid Losses

One dollar is worth more to a start-up than a million dollars is to a billion-dollar company. The most difficult financing to get, and the most expensive—if you can get it—is funding to pay for losses before you have proven your potential. That's why it does not pay to lose money at the start. You are likely to pay a high price in dilution and in loss of control, or you will pay the high price of bankruptcy if you borrow from a bank that requires a personal guarantee.

Finance-smart entrepreneurs use skills and strategies to grow without losses and to keep control of their venture. Many of the billion-dollar and hundred-million-dollar entrepreneurs avoid losses at the start by adjusting their strategy and operations to make scarce money an advantage, spending after or along with sales, keeping break-even levels lower than tested sales, seeking stage-wise returns from each dollar spent (due to the high cost of money at earlier stages), growing at the right speed, and testing key decisions before investing larger amounts.

Skills to Reduce Working Capital Needs

Working capital is tough to finance because inventory may be tough to liquidate, and accounts receivable may be tough to collect, especially in failed ventures.

VCs do offer additional rounds of financing based on performance, but with dilution to entrepreneurs. The good news is that there is not much need for inventory and accounts receivable in the digital age.

Billion-dollar entrepreneurs use a variety of strategies to reduce working capital needs.

To control inventory, they increase throughput by making operations faster and more efficient to control inventory.

Amancio Ortega of Zara started his apparel business selling bathrobes by getting materials on credit. He believed in fast turnaround to reduce inventory and working capital needs. By speeding throughput and reducing inventory, he controlled cash and grew. That's why now he is one of the world's richest men.

Billion-dollar entrepreneurs reversed cash flow by selling direct to consumers. They got paid in advance by their customers and paid on terms to their vendors. This allowed them to use their vendors as their working capital sources and increase their credit lines as their sales grew.

When he started his venture, Michael Dell financed his Dell Technologies' needs by getting terms from vendors and getting advance payments from customers.

Online furniture and home-goods store Wayfair collects money directly from its customers. And it gets terms from its suppliers.

Wayfair got extended terms from their vendors by establishing a relationship of trust and by making sure that they lived up to their end of the agreement. The extended terms allowed them to use vendor financing for growth.

Dick Schulze of Best Buy did not have the capital for his first big consumer electronics store. He got financing from his vendors, like Sony.

These billion-dollar entrepreneurs eliminated or reduced accounts receivable by seeking advances from their customers.

Entrepreneurs such as Brett Shockley of Spanlink and Rod Burwell of Xerxes also sought advances from customers. Although their corporate customers did not relish paying up front, the benefits encouraged them to do so.

Brett Shockley was one of the first entrepreneurs to develop an interactive voice response system as a way for corporations to route incoming calls to the right person and link the call to the customer's information on the corporate database. The immense benefits of cutting costs and making customers happier by reducing time allowed Spanlink to sell these benefits to corporate customers who paid upfront. Rod Burwell developed the fiberglass cover for barges. Cargill wanted the barge and offered Burwell payment up front to help fund the venture.

Billion-dollar entrepreneurs experiment and test a variety of sales drivers to find the most productive ones. These sales drivers help them increase sales at lower cost and capture the targeted market segment.

Guy Schoenecker started Business Incentives by selling engagement rings via a barber network (supposedly barbers are the first to know when men plan to propose). Gary Holmes started in business at the age of eleven by developing a network of three thousand Boy Scouts to sell light bulbs. By age sixteen, he sold the business which he had grown with sales in excess of $200,000.

When they do not have the working capital to fund their venture, billion-dollar entrepreneurs form an alliance with a corporate partner.

Richard Burke of UnitedHealth Group formed an alliance with physician groups to organize health-maintenance organizations (HMOs). The groups owned the HMO and funded it while Burke managed it. When he had developed a portfolio of HMOs, he went public and bought the HMOs he was managing.

Mike Bloomberg used an alliance with Merrill Lynch to build Bloomberg LP, his successful financial, software, data, and media company.

One key lesson from these billion-dollar entrepreneurs is to not only look at what you want to sell. If you want to grow with less, you also need to think about focusing on the right customers to cut the costs of reaching them and selling to them, get high margins, and get paid fast.

Skills to Minimize Fixed-Asset Needs

Reducing the financing needed for fixed assets is normally easier than reducing the financing needed for working capital. Fixed assets such as real estate are easier to lease at the start because it usually needs less capital for better space, and often the cost of leasing ties up less capital than owning would. Leasing may not be viable when the real estate or equipment needed is specialized.

Rather than renting fixed levels of space, Bob Kierlin of Fastenal rented garage space from local residents on an as-needed basis. Fastenal is now America's largest seller of nuts and bolts, i.e. fasteners. As noted earlier, he had to buy inventory in large quantities from Japan to get a great price. Instead of tying up his capital in a warehouse, he offered to rent garages locally on a short-term lease. When he did not need the space, he returned the garages to the homeowner.

When in need of equipment, entrepreneurs can buy or lease. But beyond looking at the monthly cost of buying or leasing, you should look at the cash needs for down payments when you buy equipment and real estate and of the potential lack of flexibility. If the equipment will not be fully utilized, consider renting as needed.

Outsourcing can also help entrepreneurs reduce fixed assets and lower their break-even levels. This enables faster profitability and take off with lower levels of cash. You can insource operations as your sales increase. But if you have strong proprietary technology where your secrets are likely to be appropriated by others, you may want to control the assets to protect your technology.

The key financial benefit of outsourcing and leasing is that it is easier to get nondilutive financing for fixed assets, and the cost to finance fixed assets is usually less than the cost for other needs.

Glenn Hasse of Ryt-Way, a sub-contract food packager, relied on customers to fund fixed assets. Dick Schulze of Best Buy relied on developers to lease the stores, as did Sam Walton of Walmart. Both Best Buy and Walmart got attractive lease rates because they were anchors. The other stores in the shopping center paid more to offset the great deals given to the anchor stores. Finance-smart entrepreneurs know not to use their own limited capital for easily financed uses such as real estate.

Skills to Grow with Positive Cash Flow

High growth with positive cash flow can be difficult to achieve. To pull this off, especially without VC, entrepreneurs need real-time management, financial skills, and the wherewithal to use these skills to beat their competitors. Bob Kierlin was able to build Fastenal into a multi-billion nuts-and-bolts dealer by being able to grow at an annual rate of 30 percent with internal cash flow. In order to do this, he owned only inventory and leased all other assets to reduce cash needs. He then focused on keeping his gross margins high by sourcing his products from around the world. He also trained his employees in-house, and this allowed the company the ability to grow at 30 percent.

Skills to Find the Right Financing at Each Stage

The venture's stage is one of the most important factors affecting financing. Early stages are higher risk, so most financiers avoid funding ventures at early stages. As the venture goes from early stage to late, risk is reduced as potential becomes more evident. That's when financing is easier to obtain.

Sam Walton was able to become the world's largest retailer and keep control through financing by stage. Initially, he obtained financing from his family to start his first few stores. When he moved to the big-box format, he continued his practice of leasing all fixed assets, using his vendors for his inventory. The fact that his customers paid when they picked up the inventory helped. When he was attractive to the public markets, he went public.

Conclusion

The key skill is real-time financial management, i.e. getting accurate financial statements in a timely fashion, and then knowing how to interpret them to avoid surprises and reach your goals. Reaching your goals while controlling your business may make you rich. Reaching without control can make other people rich.

Capital-Efficient Launch Skills

Nearly all entrepreneurs will need the skills to launch with limited cash. Those on the capital-intensive VC track need to get there with seed capital from friends, family, and angel investors and prove their potential in a high-growth, emerging industry to raise VC. Few ventures succeed on this track.

Entrepreneurs on the capital-efficient track need to launch with limited cash from friends, family, and angels, and then continue to grow while maintaining control by avoiding or delaying VC. Here are some billion-dollar entrepreneurial skills to take off with control.

Skills to Focus

Money is both expensive and scarce at the start. To keep control, entrepreneurs need to focus their efforts and their money for long-term dominance.

After Medtronic took off, it over-expanded. Bakken and his partner tried to sell the company. But there were no good offers. Consequently, Medtronic put together a new financing plan and a strong board of directors and management team to transition from an entrepreneurial venture to a professionally managed corporation. In addition to a bank loan, Medtronic secured a $200,000 investment from a VC fund that placed two people on the board. These two were experienced business professionals who insisted that Medtronic decide on the kind of company it wanted to become, encapsulate this mission in a written statement, share it with all the employees, and focus the company's scarce resources on products and markets consistent with this mission. Medtronic decided to focus on implantable therapeutic technologies (devices) that restored people to meaningful lives. In addition to the requirement of developing and writing the mission, another of the financiers' key requirements was to instill corporate discipline, which meant keeping track of all expenses and of the return for each dollar spent and hiring a comptroller who was charged with controlling costs. This new mission and plan helped Medtronic to focus, bring order, and dominate the industry it created.

Ray Barton of Great Clips decided to employ a rifle-based strategy rather than expanding without a focus. He focused on one market at a time to become the biggest hair-cutting chain in the market before considering other markets. Since franchisees had to thrive for Great Clips to succeed, Barton developed a local training center to train hair stylists, had local staff in place to support them, developed enough units in each market to pay for the investment in the training center and support staff, and offered franchisees the capacity to develop the number of units needed to saturate and dominate. Many other franchisors in the industry expected to successfully grow without a focused strategy and did not support their franchisees. They crashed.

Skills to Make Customers Happier without Capital

Finance-smart entrepreneurs need missionary sales skills to make customers happier than in their experiences with existing vendors. To do so, most sell directly to customers. Many I talked to noted that one key benefit of selling directly is that they can monitor the relationship and control it to ensure customer satisfaction.

Dick Schulze of Best Buy learned that competent and motivated salespeople who are happy with the company and can also make customers happy are key to exemplary performance when customer interaction is key. Schulze made it his priority to find such salespeople and promote them. As Schulze put it, his competitors focused on the business model, while he focused on his company's culture and people. His competitors could not steal Best Buy's culture.

Skills to Find the Right Sales Driver

Every business, especially in an emerging industry, needs to understand how to sell itself and its products cost effectively. Credibility is always crucial when selling anything. This means that you need to find the best sales driver that allows you to get the highest return—in the form of sales and cash flow—on your sales investment in the shortest time. Find it before you run out of cash.

As Medtronic started to market pacemakers, it tried a variety of sales drivers. But Bakken and Hermundslie found that it was not easy to convince conservative physicians to try their cardiac pacemaker. However, when their peers presented ground-breaking advances based on using Medtronic pacemakers at surgical conferences, physicians listened and started to use their products.

Skills to Be a PR Whiz

Publicity never hurts. Make it a priority to build relations with the press. Understand your target market and know how to reach them, whether it is in print, TV, e-marketing, etc. Excellence at what you do helps you develop a story to tell.

Horst Rechelbacher of Aveda knew how to get publicity. He knew that the press is eager to seek news about innovations that are useful to readers. He was able to generate a lot of buzz for his spa, hair-training school, and products in the local and national press. When he developed a line of organic products, he received lots of favorable publicity by taking a trip to the Amazon. Rechelbacher's rule was to "pre-tell" the press, then tell them again with a splashy event, and then follow-up with another press release, samples, and photos.

Skills to Grow at the Right Speed

As we will discuss in more detail later, there are three speeds that entrepreneurs need to consider. The first is cash flow speed—to grow at the maximum speed possible from internal cash flow, while simultaneously optimizing internal cash flow. The second is customer speed—to grow along with the market and capture customers as they are ready to buy. The third, and perhaps most important speed to avoid being left behind, is competitor speed— to grow at least as fast as direct competitors until the time when you can develop your key advantage and grow faster than your direct competitors.

Skills to Price

Pricing is one of the most important skills you need, and one of the most difficult to master for a new business. The right way to price is based on perceived value to the customer. Understand what your customers want; know your competition and the competitive value you offer. Then, **have the sales skills to price to value**.

One great example is Richard Burke of UnitedHealth who developed his business so consumers could keep their existing physicians, which allowed him to charge a premium price compared to the competition.

Skills to Dominate Emerging Trends

Of all the skills, this could be the most important. Among Minnesota's billion- and hundred-million-dollar entrepreneurs, 96 percent jump on an emerging trend and dominate it. Nationally, billion-dollar entrepreneurs, from Bill Gates and Steve Jobs to Marc Zuckerberg and Travis Kalanick, all do the same. It is easier to soar with the trends than against the current. But you need to develop the skills in the emerging industry.

Bakken of Medtronic found his company at the confluence of great trends. Society was willing to accept the implanting of man-made technologies to extend and enrich human life. Technology advanced rapidly in the fields of electronics and integrated circuits, materials, batteries, and other areas to make pacemakers smaller, longer lasting, and more effective. Additionally, clinical experience and innovative physicians helped to identify other areas in the human body that could use this new technology. And government in the form of Medicare helped a large number of older patients to take advantage of these new technologies, thus dynamically expanding the market. As a result, Medtronic took off.

Skills to Track the Business in Real Time

Launching the business in real time is like an airplane taking off from a limited runway. You need to take off before running out of cash, especially if you cannot raise more. Tracking the business allows you to know what is happening, monitor for potential problems, and take care of the problems before they sink the business.

Don Kotula of Northern Tool tested assumptions and tracked the business in real time to avoid surprises. He tracked his advertising and results, referrals, and sales. One of the important tests he conducted was to find the right pricing strategy. When he started Northern Tool, he compared prices for similar new equipment from the vendors, checked the Sears and Wards catalogs, and called competitors to determine their prices. He found that his kits had to be about 30 to 40 percent below the price of assembled equipment.

Tracking the business in real time is crucial to know what is happening. Otherwise, you are flying blind.

Skills to Adjust Based on Real Feedback

Entrepreneurs have pivoted since long before the word became fashionable. Testing before launch will not remove uncertainty completely. There are always unknowns—especially in growing ventures and emerging industries. This means that entrepreneurs need to launch, test, and adjust. When you find what works, that's the time to go all in.

ADJUST TO MARKET REALITY: When your initial idea does not work, which happens frequently in new ventures, talk to your customers and adapt to what the market demands. After finishing his MBA, Bob Kierlin of Fastenal spent two years in the Peace Corps and then started to work for IBM. But his dream since high school was to develop a vending machine to sell nuts and bolts. In 1967, he and three friends raised $22,000 and developed a vending machine to sell fasteners. This vision, which had been gestating for many years, produced a concept that did not last long. The quantities and sizes demanded by customers were not the same as the ones planned for the vending machine. Kierlin scrapped the vending-machine strategy. He developed a retail store in the same space and hired a store manager while he continued to work at IBM.

ADJUST TO NEW TRENDS: Sam Walton spent twelve years searching for the right formula to grow in small towns. When he heard about two Ben Franklin stores that were laid out for self-service, with cash registers at the exit and not throughout the store, he copied it for his own store, as did others like Target and Kmart.[3] This trend changed retailing because it allowed for better inventory control with fewer employees.

ADJUST TO NEW INSIGHTS: Travis Kalanick and Garrett Camp started Uber as a limo rental service. They soon realized that they could link people needing more affordable rides with people willing to give the rides. That adjustment helped Uber take off.

ADJUST TO NEW OPPORTUNITIES: When Bill Gates and Paul Allen started Microsoft, their plan was not to sell operating systems. But when Gates found that IBM wanted an operating system, he found one, bought it, and licensed it to IBM.

ADJUST TO TAKE OFF: When your venture shows promise, adjust to the new reality. When Mark Zuckerberg was a Harvard freshman, he started Facebook as a Harvard-only enterprise. Facebook eventually grew to include membership for students from other schools. When Facebook really took off, Peter Thiel went to Boston, offered an investment in Facebook, and encouraged Zuckerberg to move to Silicon Valley.

ADJUST AFTER LAUNCH: As with many new technologies, once the initial barrier has been broken, many improvements are introduced. At Medtronic, other teams started coming up with new applications and new technologies to add to Bakken's cardiac pacemaker. This is when Medtronic heard about the battery-powered Chardack-Greatbatch implantable pacemaker that allowed longer-term pacing, more convenience, and fewer surgical complications. Medtronic licensed the technology on an exclusive basis. Medtronic continues to track advances, form alliances, and license or acquire new technologies.

ADJUST BASED ON NEW INFORMATION: When the market points in a different direction, pivot. When Horst Rechelbacher of Aveda opened his salons, he trained hairdressers in his groundbreaking techniques from Europe. But after they were trained, the hairdressers wanted a bigger cut and other salons succeeded in recruiting them. Horst then sold his salons and opened a training school. He wrote to those who had hired his trained designers and asked them to send him others who wanted to be trained. He got more than he could handle.

Conclusion

Take off is difficult. Develop the skills to price, sell, grow, and monitor. Then, launch and adjust.

Summary: Corporate, VC, and Entrepreneurial Financing

How do the finance strategies of billion-dollar entrepreneurs differ from those of corporations and VCs? Here is a thumbnail summary of the differences in the three types of financing that seek growth, assuming that your goal is not to stay small.

Table 1: Risk vs Internal Rate of Return (IRR) Comparisons

Higher Target IRR	Venture Capital	Billion-Dollar Entrepreneurs
Lower Target IRR	Small Business	Corporations
	Higher Risk	**Lower Risk**

💰 **VENTURE CAPITAL:**

- ▸ VCs take more risks than corporations and billion-dollar entrepreneurs and expect higher returns.

- ▸ The most important factor affecting VC investing is exit, i.e. timing and valuation. VCs are happiest when exits are fast and for the highest valuation. They need to exit from their ventures since their funds have a limited life.

- ▸ Money is their advantage and is used to control the venture, especially if you need more of it and they can offer it.

- ▸ VCs finance in stages. They invest more in later stages if projections are achieved and potential is still there. The valuation of the venture increases at each succeeding stage.

- ▸ Expect many failures for early-stage VC portfolios.

- ‣ VCs often finance in syndicates to reduce their portfolio risk and increase portfolio potential by investing in their partners' ventures.
- ‣ Bootstrap: not after their investment. VCs expect ventures to pursue a high-growth, capital-intensive strategy.
- ‣ Structure: all equity financing.
- ‣ Terms: favorable to VCs by allowing VCs to control the venture's direction, strategy, and leadership.

💰 **CORPORATIONS:**

- ‣ Money is there, but tough to get due to the need to reduce risk.
- ‣ Corporations accept (and expect) lower annual returns than VCs.
- ‣ Bootstrap: may have to do to get to next stage where start-ups can show potential and reduce risk.
- ‣ Corporations often like consistency in their financial structures, which includes levels of debt and equity and payback periods.
- ‣ Amounts: Corporations can invest large amounts if able to show potential and reduce risk.

💰 **BILLION-DOLLAR ENTREPRENEURS**

- ‣ Capital efficiency: The key principle is to spend to make customers happier. Lean elsewhere to grow more with less until Aha, when more capital is available and can be controlled.
- ‣ They bootstrap before Aha to reduce needs and are capital-smart after Aha to find the right amounts of capital from the right sources to control the venture and dominate the industry.

- Investment happens in small amounts with entrepreneurs seeking internal cash flow to balance internal and external financing.

- Structure: Financing should balance risk and return, and balance cash flow, debt, and equity. Debt should be within limits of cash flow repayment capacity, especially in the early stages when VC is very controlling. This can be key to retaining control and reducing risk.

- Sources: First internal cash flow; then nonfinancial sources that don't seek equity or personal guarantees; then debt; then low-dilution equity; then VC if there's no other choice.

- Amounts: Low based on low needs (due to controlled growth rate and low-risk spending) and high internal cash flow.

- Key to terms: Retain control.

Part II

Finance: Financing Growth

99.98 percent of entrepreneurs will not get VC or will fail with VC. The remaining 0.02 percent can control their venture and the wealth they create by delaying VC. While avoiding or delaying VC, entrepreneurs can evaluate their options and improve their odds of success by using the right strategy, structure, sources, and instruments for each stage.

Raising money for a new business or a growing venture is one of the most difficult aspects of business. Where you see potential, financiers see risk. To succeed at raising the right financing, it helps to know how others see your venture and the financing options open to you.

In Silicon Valley, some billion-dollar entrepreneurs use VC to build capital-intensive ventures. Most of them delay VC till there is proof of venture potential and leadership skills and thereby control the venture. Outside Silicon Valley, billion-dollar entrepreneurs tend to be capital efficient and mainly grow without VC.

This chapter shows how billion-dollar entrepreneurs finance their ventures to grow with control.

What Venture Capitalists Do

Early-stage VC funds raise money from institutional investors to invest in high-potential ventures that can dominate emerging industries.

VC Works for Few

Because of the risk, the institutional investors who finance VC funds want to earn high annual returns of more than 20 percent. This return is difficult to get due to the large proportion of failing ventures in a VC portfolio. To pay for the failing ventures and earn the desired portfolio returns, VCs need home runs, and home runs are few. This need for incredibly successful ventures makes the VC strategy work well for the top four percent of VCs—nearly all of whom are in Silicon Valley—and mainly when high-potential industries are emerging.

VCs Use High-Risk Equity Instruments

Silicon Valley VC funds offer equity financing to early-stage ventures that seek to grow at a rapid pace and when cash flow is usually negative. This means that the venture is a high-risk investment and many of the ventures fail. In addition to the venture risk, Silicon Valley VCs also invest in these ventures using high-risk equity instruments such as preferred stock. They don't demand collateral and personal guarantees, unlike bankers. This means that when the venture fails, VCs lose money. To have a successful portfolio, early-stage VC funds need a few home runs. Without home runs, early-stage VCs fail.

VC Funds Invest Large Amounts per Venture

In recent years, VC funds have become huge. To be able to manage their portfolio efficiently and effectively, VCs invest large amounts in a limited number of ventures. The larger and more successful Silicon Valley VCs are interested in home-run ventures that need large amounts of capital and give them a high return. But ventures that need large amounts of capital and give high returns to VCs can result in significant dilution to the entrepreneurs.

What Finance-Smart Entrepreneurs Do

Finance-smart entrepreneurs grow with control. They control the venture and the wealth they create. To build high-potential ventures without VC or with delayed VC, finance-smart entrepreneurs use the following strategies:

💰 Prove bottom-up assumptions

- 💰 Focus on cash flow till Aha
- 💰 Finance appropriately to the stage
- 💰 Channel equity
- 💰 Use Alt-VC first
- 💰 Seek scalable debt
- 💰 Choose smarter instruments
- 💰 Use VC intelligently
- 💰 Develop the right capital structure

Chapter 4

Prove Bottom-Up Assumptions

The problem with new ventures is risk. Entrepreneurs have faith that the venture will succeed. Financiers are usually skeptical. Since nearly everything at this stage is an unknown, it is difficult to raise money until you prove your assumptions. This suggests that you should develop bottom-up assumptions, and then prove them.

If you manage your business without knowing your numbers, you are very likely to fail. To control your business, you need to know what you are expecting and what you are achieving. Your financial projections are your hopes. Your financial statements are your reality.

New businesses, even well-managed ones, usually fail to project accurately in at least two key areas.

The first is the level and timing of revenues, where entrepreneurs usually are too optimistic. The most important number in developing financial projections for any new venture is your sales projections. This number influences many aspects of a business, including strategy, resources, investment, and costs. And this is a number that will nearly always be wrong in a start-up, unless you are a contract vendor with a fixed contract.

The second and equally important number to forecast is the investment required to achieve sales targets. This is your cost of sales and marketing. As a new business, you are not known to customers, and they may be reluctant to take the risk of buying from you. You also don't know the right sales driver, the productivity of the sales driver, and the investment you need to make in the sales driver in order to achieve the level of sales expected. Existing companies have historical experience that tells them how much they should spend on sales and marketing. Startups have no such history.

Even though sales projections for startups are nearly always wrong, that the real reason to develop these projections is to forecast the relationship between the investment in your sales driver and your sales to monitor your results and examine variances, to adjust before you go broke.

The other numbers in your financial projections are, or should be, a function of your expected sales. This includes the cost of goods sold and your overhead. You should be using or investing in assets based on your anticipated sales. So, focus on developing reasonable projections for sales and how you will get sales. For reasonable projections, seek bottom-up projections.

Top-Down v. Bottom-Up Projections

Entrepreneurs can develop their financial projections in two ways: top-down or bottom-up.

TOP-DOWN PROJECTIONS: You start by estimating the size of the total market and then forecasting your estimated market share. This gives a forecast of revenues. Existing businesses who have a history should be able to calculate their market shares in previous years and extrapolate this data to project their market share in the future.

New ventures have no such history and any assumptions about market share are likely to be wrong. New ventures in emerging industries have two problems—they don't have a good basis to forecast the size of the industry since there is limited history, and they don't have a good basis to estimate market share. Market research may help, but market research is of limited use in emerging industries where everyone is guessing.

BOTTOM-UP PROJECTIONS: New ventures, and businesses seeking to improve their sales and marketing effectiveness, should find the right sales driver, determine the right amount to be spent on this sales driver, and estimate the expected sales based on bottom-up projections.

Your sales driver is the right strategy you will employ to get sales, such as whether you will use sales personnel, print advertising, online advertising, etc. In a new venture, you first need to spend money to get sales since you have no market share. Bottom-up forecasting starts with evaluating alternate sales drivers based on your industry practices and sales drivers that are targeted to your target customer segment.

Here's why bottom-up projections are better for entrepreneurs than top-down projections.

Bottom-Up Projections Help Better Estimate Cost, Revenues, and Time to Revenues

Bottom-up sales forecasting requires that you know the cost to reach potential customers and estimate how many will buy and the time it will take them to make the decision to buy and act on it. The attractiveness of your value proposition is likely to determine how long it takes for customers to switch to you. Your value proposition and the time and cost to get customers can vary with their knowledge about your product, your product's relative advantage, the cost to switch, the complexity to understand and use your product, your warranties, and the ease of buying the product. Bottom-up projections allow you to test these variables to see how they affect the buying decision, to make changes to find the right sales driver, to decide the right levels of investment in these sales drivers, and use the right estimates for sales.

Lloyd Sigel of Lloyd's BBQ introduced fully cooked vacuum-packed barbequed ribs into the consumer market in the late 1970s. Due to the newness of the product, he was unsure of the right pricing, the right promotion, or the anticipated sales level. So, he tested various options for packaging, pricing, and stores to find what worked before developing his final projections.

Bottom-Up Sales Forecast Helps at the Start Prior to History

Sales are usually slow at the start because potential customers may not have heard of you and may not want to buy from a new company. In high-growth companies, sales grow—if they do grow—in the shape of a hockey stick: slow at the start, and faster after you have learned to sell and after the market has accepted your product. Bottom-up sales projections help to better monitor your actual performance and adjust as, and when, needed.

Jill Blashack Strahan of Tastefully Simple kept costs low and inventory under control so the company would have a positive cash flow even with low levels of sales. Tastefully Simple's initial product line included twenty-two products with an average price of $5.95 in a simple, well-designed brochure with line illustrations of the products. All the food products were specially chosen to fit Jill Blashack Strahan's goal of being either "open-and-enjoy" or not requiring more than two ingredients to prepare. Several products were privately labeled for Tastefully Simple.

Once she had her inventory, Strahan was ready to have her first home taste-testing party. Her original goal was to have twelve people at each party and an average sale of twenty-five dollars per person. She was also expecting one or two people at each party to offer to host additional gatherings. She expected to have five salespeople by the end of the first year. At her first party, her sales totaled two hundred dollars to five customers. Fewer customers bought, but the average sale was higher. Most importantly, four wanted to host parties. From this start, Tastefully Simple has grown to more than 28,000 sales consultants nationwide. To get hosts, Strahan started with people she knew. They invited their friends, and her business snowballed. The marketing was based on word of mouth at the grassroots level. She packed orders on a pool table. Her partner who had another day job installed software and entered orders at night. All sales were for cash up front, and Strahan had to pay for her inventory in thirty to forty-five days. Watching inventory and overhead, she had a positive cash flow quickly, even with a low sales level.

Bottom-Up Testing Leads to Efficient and Cost-Effective Ways to Reach Customers

Existing companies usually know how to sell. They know which sales drivers work and the productivity of each. Entrepreneurs need to find the most cost-effective sales driver to sell at the lowest cost and produce cash flow quickly. Testing alternative sales drivers helps you find the right one for you. Then, you need to determine the right amount to be spent on the sales driver based on your resources and goals, including the right level of sales, profits, cash flow, and other key metrics for your venture. Lastly, you monitor your actual sales and sales driver productivity, and you adjust your business.

Aveda's Horst Rechelbacher realized from personal experience that there was a large unmet need for hairdresser training when he started losing the hairstylists he had trained at high cost to himself. He decided to fill this need by starting a hairdressers' training school. Rechelbacher sent a letter to all salon operators in a five-state area, especially in Minnesota's Minneapolis-St. Paul, asking for referrals while reminding them that they had benefited significantly by hiring his trained hairdressers. He was going to help them even more by committing to providing excellent training for their stylists at his school. His initial break-even level was thirty-five. He got forty-five students in his first class. He did not have to spend money on expensive advertising and promotion to get students. He had positive cash flow immediately.

John Wanamaker, pioneering department store executive, noted, "*half the money I spend on advertising is wasted; the trouble is, I don't know which half.*"[4] Advertising campaigns are not predictable. New ventures that rely on a massive ad campaign to succeed are taking a huge risk due to the lack of predictability in new businesses and the risky nature of advertising.

Ed Flaherty of Rapid Oil Change was unsure about promoting his quick oil-change service. He tested various media to see what worked. He realized that he needed to promote in two ways.

To attract traffic, Flaherty focused on local marketing with direct mail, door-to-door coupons, and advertising in the local suburban newspaper. He measured his investment and the sales and margin returns from each media investment, eliminating ones that did not work and adding to those that did.

He also needed to build his brand throughout the metro area so that customers would not only learn of his business, but also feel comfortable using his services. By brand building through mass media such as radio and TV, he attracted higher-margin customers.

Knowing the return from every dollar spent on each sales driver can help cut the poor ones so you can focus resources on the ones that work.

Salespeople are "great gossipers," according to Guy Schoenecker of BI, a $500 million business-incentives marketer. To expand from his initial diamond business, Schoenecker talked to his customers and found that many of them were renting apartments and looking for furniture. To sell more products to existing customers, Schoenecker opened a furniture store. Schoenecker avoided advertising in the major newspapers when his tests indicated that his ads did not draw enough business to pay for the cost of the advertising. His friends who were selling advertising to large furniture retailers also found that their ads in the newspapers were "hit and miss," with some ads doing well and others failing. Schoenecker could not afford to gamble, so he focused on a sales driver that worked for him, which was direct mail. He developed a monthly direct mail flyer that helped him generate business in the first two weeks of each month, and he delivered the items in the last two weeks.

Credibility is always crucial when selling a product, and especially critical when the product involves human life. Bottom-up sales-driver analysis helps you understand what works best for you when credibility is key.

As Medtronic started to market the cardiac pacemaker that cofounder Earl Bakken had developed, it tried a variety of sales drivers, including distributors, reps, internal sales personnel, and trade shows. However, Bakken and his partner, Palmer Hermundslie, found it difficult to convince conservative physicians, hospitals, and insurance companies to use their pacemakers. Bakken found that physicians started avoiding Medtronic at medical association meetings. However, when other physicians including Dr. C. Walton Lillehei (the first customer who requested the pacemaker) and Dr. William M. Chardack (who codeveloped the battery that made the implanted pacemaker possible), presented their ground-breaking advances based on Medtronic pacemakers at medical conferences, other physicians listened and started using their products. Physicians were willing to listen to leaders in their own profession, but not to entrepreneurs trying to "sell" them a product. The lesson here is this: find the best sales driver for the highest return on your sales investment in the shortest time.

Bottom-Up Selling Connects Sales Expenses to Sales

The key financial elements of a business plan for a start-up venture include sales, gross margins, expenses, and cash flow. Entrepreneurs need to generate sales cost effectively since the cost of sales and marketing can be huge and their productivity uncertain at the start. Reducing this cost and the uncertainty is crucial to entrepreneurial success.

Guy Schoenecker of BI got his start by selling diamonds for rings to GIs in his college. After World War II, when the GIs were entering college under the GI bill, Schoenecker decided to focus on this market to pay his own way through college. He spread the word to colleges in the area by placing ads in school newspapers. But ads cost money, and Schoenecker was looking for more cost-effective and direct ways to build his business. In talking with his barber, he realized that barbers were the information centers of the neighborhood—the Facebook of the pre-Internet era. He started calling on area barbers and offered them a commission. He joined various clubs to spread the word. When Schoenecker asked his customers how they had heard of him, he found that his most productive sales driver was word of mouth. Satisfied customers spread the word. Schoenecker focused on customer service, and after his business started growing, he stopped advertising, having found that ad prospects were more cautious than referrals.

Bottom-Up Selling Is More Conducive to Testing

Few, if any, can predict what will work in a new venture. Everyone is guessing—even with market research. The best entrepreneurs test various sales drivers and evaluate the resulting sales per dollar spent on marketing. Relying on experts, especially those like ad agencies who collect their money based on your expenses, can be dangerous to the venture.

Steve Shank wanted Capella to have a national image and reputation when he started the company in the late 1990s. But Capella had very little money for national image advertising, and the early objective was to learn what worked and what did not. Shank wanted to generate leads for enrollments, and he wanted to do it cost effectively. He tried print media such as the *New York Times*, but the results did not meet expectations. So early on, he tested results from online advertising, including through sites such as AOL. Capella was the early adopter of online ads in post-secondary education. The strategy worked.

Bottom-Up Selling Helps to Target Market

Know where and how to find your customers. If you spend too much money and time finding the right customers, you could fail before you have a chance at success. The key is to know who your customers are and how to reach them most effectively and efficiently.

Don Kotula of Northern Tool coded every ad and every catalog and tracked the resulting prospects, customers, and their lifetime sales by the ad and the magazine that first attracted them. In doing so, he gathered information about his customers, what they buy, how much they buy, and how profitable they are for his company. This showed him that catalogs are better than ads, that ads in July don't work, and that there is a high degree of correlation between those who like tools, those who fish, and those who buy cabins. He developed his own mailing lists from his ads and got customers' addresses from their checks. He would encourage his customers to refer friends to receive a catalog, and most of them were happy to do so. This helped Kotula expand his mailing list without a high cost. By coding each ad and catalog and tracking the results, Kotula gets returns of 10 percent. Many companies expect only a 3 to 7 percent return on their mailings.

Conclusion

Many corporations, academics, and consultants plan from the top down with the development of visions, mission statements, strategies, and tactics. Billion-dollar entrepreneurs are more practical. They know that their venture's vision is cloudy, the strategy to dominate is unclear, and that they may have to pivot to find the key to success. As Al Ries and Jack Trout have noted in their books on marketing, entrepreneurs should *go from tactics to strategy and not from strategy to tactics*. This means you need to know what works (tactics) and then develop the strategy based on the tactics that work. After finding what works, improve your forecasts and start to expand.

To grow more with less, focus on bottom-up projections. This means analyzing what you have to do to get sales to find the best sales driver. Then, analyze how much you have to spend to get the target level of sales. And then, monitor the actual results to make sure that you are not going in the wrong direction.

Chapter 5

Focus on Cash Flow Until Aha

Aha is when you don't have to promise potential—the world can see it. Till Aha, no one returns your calls. After Aha, VCs come knocking on your door. Before Aha, your cost of money is very high, and you could lose control. After Aha, you may be able to write your own terms. So be frugal and focus on positive cash flow till Aha. After Aha, select the right strategy that works for you.

As I've mentioned before, VCs invest in a few ventures after they show promise of potential. And yet they fail on most of their ventures. To earn a high return from a portfolio that will have many failures, VCs need some evidence of high potential before they will consider investing in the venture, i.e. they need Aha. This means that entrepreneurs need to build their ventures from idea till Aha with limited cash.

VCs Invest after Aha

Aha is that magic moment when potential is evident—you don't have to promise it. Before Aha, VC is scarce. After Aha, it is usually easier to get VC. Since ventures need to reach Aha with limited funds, entrepreneurs should be careful with pre-Aha capital. Here are the Aha stages you should consider.

PRE-AHA STAGE: At start-up, entrepreneurs often write business plans and seek equity financing from VCs. About 99.8 percent of startups will not get VC. They mostly end up getting money from family and friends.

OPPORTUNITY-AHA STAGE: This is the stage when the advantage in your product, service, or technology may be evident, but you have not yet developed the right business strategy for dominance nor proven yourself. Assuming you are able to convince VCs to invest in your venture, your negotiating clout may be minimal, you are likely to be diluted, and you may have to cede control of your venture to the VCs. If the venture becomes a home run, you are likely to do well. David Huber got $300 million from Ciena, the company he created, even though he was fired.[5] Herb Boyer, the coinventor of the gene-splicing technique and codeveloper of Genentech, is another good example of an entrepreneur who benefited from his invention. A VC from Silicon Valley joined with Boyer to start one of the first billion-dollar corporations of the biotechnology era. If the venture does not become a home run, you may not see much benefit, and you will have lost control of your one great opportunity.

BUSINESS-AHA STAGE: At this stage, your business is taking off because you have found the right strategy. Your business has momentum and investors are more eager to fund you than in previous stages. In addition to valuation, the key question is about leadership—whether to keep you as the leader or hire a professional executive as the CEO. Entrepreneurs who got VC funding at this stage and did not retain control include Pierre Omidyar of eBay and Steve Jobs of Apple.

LEADERSHIP-AHA STAGE: This is when the venture's potential and your leadership skills are evident. If you are in Silicon Valley or in a hot emerging industry, VCs may be chasing you. That means you get to select the VCs who are right for you. Most importantly, you keep control of your venture.

The founders of Google,[6] Facebook[7], and Snapchat[8] demanded super-voting rights and controlled their venture, even with VC. In one of the most unusual VC arrangements, Mark Zuckerberg of Facebook was able to control his investors and vote their shares rather than the other way around. He owned about 28 percent of Facebook. But he demanded voting rights from his investors, and these rights gave him control of about 57 percent of the company.[9] VCs went along with his demands because they could smell a home run.

VCS ARE PICKY: VCs fund ventures that will provide the VCs with a high return, i.e. ventures that demonstrate evidence of potential to dominate high-potential, emerging industries. There are very few ventures that show this potential. To get VC, your venture needs to stand out. One way to do so is to show proof of potential.

Kleiner Perkins rejected Steve Jobs's request for funding when Apple was a start-up. He liked to understand the risk so he could try to eliminate it. He has noted that *"my idea in everything has been to put the risk up front and get rid of the risk as fast as you possibly can."*[10] Perkins could not see the genius of Steve Jobs by looking into his eyes.

When the strategic alliance with a giant company did not work, Steve Shank of Capella University sought alternate growth financing. VCs liked what they saw in the company and offered an investment of $40 million to $100 million when the company only wanted to raise $15 million. Note that it is easier to obtain VC when entrepreneurs have proof of potential. Shank picked the VC whose terms fit his needs.

Start-up ventures seldom receive VC if their competitive edge and high potential are not evident. It is difficult to get VC funding for a start-up venture that does not have a revolutionary technology, or where the entrepreneur does not have a track record of success from a previous venture.

Dell Computer did not receive VC because there was nothing that distinguished Michael Dell or his company from his competitors. Dell tapped family resources for his initial capital and grew without the need for external cash.[11] His business model had a reverse cash-flow cycle where he got cash from his customers before he had to pay his vendors. The more he sold, the more cash he had in the bank.

SOURCE OF THE ADVANTAGE: The source of a venture's competitive advantage can affect how VCs view its attractiveness. When the competitive advantage is in the technology or strategy and there is demonstrable evidence that this gives the venture an edge in a high-potential industry, VCs are likely to invest. They may also recruit experienced CEOs.

But if the competitive advantage is the skill of the entrepreneur, VCs may not be convinced to invest until after momentum has been established. Sixty-eight percent of the ventures in the Minnesota study succeeded solely due to the skills of the entrepreneur. They did not get VC.

IMPLICATIONS: Few VCs invest before evidence of potential. If you are expecting to dominate your industry based on your skills, you may be forced to grow with late-VC or no VC. If you can build your venture to Aha without VC, the question is: Can you continue to grow without VC?

Odds of VC Do Not Improve at Later Stages

Are your odds better at later stages? At later stages, VCs tend to invest more money, but in fewer ventures. In 2016, VC funding ranged from $2 billion in the early stage to $20 billion in the late stage, but in fewer deals. So, you may be able to show potential, but still not get VC.

IMPLICATIONS: Most entrepreneurs will never receive VC, and securing VC does not guarantee success. All it means is that you may have ceded control of your venture to investors whose interests may not coincide with yours. Secondly, even with VC, you may not make a fortune. Instead, you may lose control of your venture. So focus on cash flow till Aha.

VC Is More Dilutive and Controlling in Earlier Stages

Since the risk is higher in earlier stages, VCs seek a reduced target annual return as a venture advances from idea to Aha, when risk is lower and more VC is available. This means that the target annual return can be as high as 80 to 100 percent per year for VC at the research and development stage and as "low" as 30 percent per year when the venture has advanced to the growth stage. At the research stage, all the risks exist from the development of the product to growth. At the growth stage, the main risks are whether the venture will continue to grow and be able to offer a very attractive exit for the VCs.

The higher risk, murky outlook, and unproven potential of both the venture and the entrepreneur in the early stages also means that the VCs demand more control over the venture. As the venture progresses to later stages and the venture's and entrepreneur's potential are more evident, VCs are usually less demanding. Entrepreneurs such as Bill Gates (Microsoft), Mark Zuckerberg (Facebook), and Jan Koum (WhatsApp) were able to keep total control by leading their ventures to the growth stage before agreeing to accept venture capital. They kept control.

By moving the company forward to the later stages without VC, entrepreneurs get to keep more of the company. Focus on capital efficiency and cash flow till the later stages when VC seeks lower returns and requires less of the company.

Conclusion

Because 99.9 percent of ventures will not get VC, entrepreneurs need to focus on capital-efficient growth.

80 percent of ventures that do get VC end up failing anyway. These ventures may have done better without VC by focusing on capital-efficient growth.

The 20 percent of entrepreneurs that succeed with VC can control the venture and reduce dilution by reaching leadership Aha before seeking VC.

Focus on cash flow till Aha! After Aha, evaluate your options.

Chapter 6

Finance to the Stage

The earlier the stage, the higher the risk. Entrepreneurs
have fewer financing options in earlier stages and any
funding obtained is expensive. To grow and keep control
in early stages, entrepreneurs should use capital efficiency
in order to reduce needs, increase internal cash flow,
and seek more from non-controlling sources. At later
stages, entrepreneurs have more options, especially if
there is evidence of potential to dominate in high-growth
emerging industries.

Billion-dollar entrepreneurs control their venture and keep more
of the wealth created by delaying or avoiding VC. To delay or
avoid VC, entrepreneurs need to know how to finance by stage.

Early-stage VC is expensive in terms of potential loss of control
and of financial dilution. As the venture gains momentum, it has
more credibility and is more likely to attract VCs if it can show the
potential to dominate the right industries. The added credibility
helps entrepreneurs negotiate from a stronger position and
continue to lead.

Venture stages range from research and development to
the growth stage. It is usually easier and cheaper to obtain

financing, whether equity or debt, in the growth stage than in the research stage.

Stages and Availability

There are four key stages in the life of a high-growth venture (Figure 4).

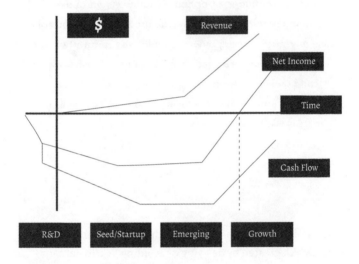

Figure 4. Stages of a Venture

RESEARCH & DEVELOPMENT (R&D) STAGE: The stage during which you are developing your initial product is the most difficult and expensive to finance. At this stage, it is impossible to independently assess the technology or the market aspects of your product or service because it does not exist except on paper. It helps if you have a track record in the technology behind the opportunity or a track record of successful technology developments. Investors may want a return as high as 100 percent per year at this stage. Even at that rate, VC at this stage is hard to get due to risk. This means that entrepreneurs need to focus on all the finance sources discussed in this book.

SEED/START-UP STAGE: In the seed-start-up stages, the venture has a product that is ready for sale, i.e. all research and development has been done and the product/service is ready for sale to customers. At the seed-start-up stage, the venture is developing its business plan. Investors can independently verify your product or service and know exactly what you plan to sell without relying on the promises of the R&D stage. Target annual returns for VCs can range from 60–80 percent. There are more investors at this stage than at the R&D stage. But the numbers are still small. Billion-dollar entrepreneurs at this stage mainly used their own savings, along with debt, leases, customer advances, alliances, and non-VC equity sources, without the risk of losing control of the business.

EMERGING STAGE: At this stage, the venture has sales with losses and negative cash flow. Cash is required to fund losses and the growing need for assets. However, since the venture has customers, investors can evaluate market acceptance, the segments, product satisfaction, and growth rates to estimate venture value. Risk is lower than in previous stages. At this stage, targeted annual returns for VCs are usually around 40 to 60 percent and up. At this stage, many of the VCs are interested because the potential of both the venture and entrepreneur are more evident. Entrepreneurs such as Gates, Bezos, and Zuckerberg got VC at this stage. But most billion-dollar entrepreneurs grew without VC at any stage by using most of the sources mentioned in this book. Their key source was a self-funding business strategy where they got paid before they had to pay. Entrepreneurs using this strategy include Dell, Schulze (Best Buy), Burke (UnitedHealth), and Walton (Walmart).

GROWTH STAGE: At this stage, the venture is growing and profitable, but may have a negative cash flow if it is growing at very high rates in order to dominate its industry. This stage is attractive to investors due to the venture's proven potential. But investors can still be blindsided by unforeseen risks. Raising funds at this stage is easier than in previous stages. The target annual return for VCs at this stage is around 25 percent and up. All sources are available at this stage, including the potential of an initial public offering if the entrepreneur is so inclined. When billion-dollar entrepreneurs got VC, they did go public to give their investors an attractive exit.

The venture's stage has a major impact on the availability of VC, the cost, and the terms. There are more VCs in later rounds than in earlier ones.

VC Is Tough to Get Before Aha

Before Aha, entrepreneurs are unlikely to get VC. About 96 percent to 98 percent of VC is provided after the first round, i.e. after Aha. After the opportunity's potential is evident, VCs may require a change in leadership as a condition for investing. After leadership Aha, VCs likely won't require that the entrepreneur cede the CEO's position to a professional executive.

Bill Gates, Jeff Bezos, and Mark Zuckerberg are billion-dollar entrepreneurs who got VC after leadership Aha, when they could show evidence that they would dominate their industry. They did get VC and stayed in control of their venture.

Financing Options Before Aha

Since it is difficult to get VC before Aha, you need to know how to get to Aha without VC. This means using a variety of strategies and sources including:

- 💰 Developing the right strategy to grow with capital efficiency.

- 💰 Proving your business potential through sales or contracts.

- 💰 Developing skills to build a growth business.

- 💰 Focusing on cash flow by cutting frills and expenses that don't lead to an immediate positive cash flow. Your financial options will increase after Aha. More importantly, your cost of money will fall.

- 💰 Using your own equity for hard-to-finance uses, such as losses, which few want to fund.

- 💰 Using VC sources that don't demand control. These may not be well-known, may be difficult to find, and the amount you raise may be smaller—but that could be the price to stay in control of your venture and the wealth it can create.

- 💰 Seeking scalable debt, which is debt that can be repaid from cash flow and is available in increasing amounts as the business grows.

- 💰 Assessing the various financial instruments to find the best fit to stay in control by reducing risk for financiers while increasing options for you.

- 💰 Using the capital raised with care and caution.

Mike Bloomberg of Bloomberg LP had a capital-intense strategy but got his funding from his own savings and from a strategic alliance with Merrill Lynch. His alliance with Merrill Lynch not only gave him his capital, but Merrill Lynch also became his first customer. After proving the value of his terminals and network at Merrill Lynch, Bloomberg had no problems getting other customers in the financial world to pay him his attractive monthly fee and helped him dominate the financial networking market. Over the years, as Merrill Lynch sold off its shares, Bloomberg acquired more and is currently said to own more than 80 percent of the company. This is the foundation for Mike Bloomberg's considerable fortune.

Seek VC if...

More than 90 percent of billion-dollar entrepreneurs grew by avoiding or delaying VC. But most VC Avoiders did not have direct competitors with VC. If your direct competitors have VC, consider getting it, but do so after leadership Aha. Consider getting it to avoid being handicapped with fewer resources than your competitors. Do so after leadership Aha so that the VCs do not seek to replace you with a professional CEO, as happened to Steve Jobs.

Michael Dell is one of the few billion-dollar entrepreneurs who beat direct competitors even though they were the ones who had VC. Ventures that are able to attract venture capital are often able to beat ventures without VC because they can use their greater resources to dominate. It is like having a bigger army. Dell was able to win because of his "not-so-secret" weapon. He had a better business strategy of selling directly to consumers. By doing so, he was able to get customers' cash before he bought the inventory and was able to generate more cash as he grew. The others built finished goods inventory and tried to sell them through retail channels, which was a very capital-intensive strategy.

Conclusion

It is crucial to find the right financing at each stage to grow with control.[ii] Knowing your financing options at each stage can help you find the right financing to grow and stay in control of your business. Grow without VC if you can, and delay VC if you need it to dominate. If you can bootstrap without VC until you have a proven product and strategy, you will increase your chances of success. If you can reach Aha, more VCs are likely to reach out to you due to higher potential and lower risk, and the best part is that you can stay in control. To get VC, the best strategy is to make them come to you.

---

ii   For more on venture financing, see "Finance Any Business Intelligently" and "Handbook of Business Finance"; www.uEntrepreneurs.com

Chapter 7

Channel Your Equity

Entrepreneurs are expected to invest a significant portion
of their assets in the venture before investors will consider
an investment in it. Investors are also more interested in
funding the less risky needs with lower-risk instruments.
This means that you will need to target your equity to the
hard-to-finance needs and higher risk instruments.

The "traditional" financing strategy for high-growth ventures has
been to secure initial financing from family and friends, followed
by angels, early-stage VCs, late-stage VCs, and an IPO. This has
been the preferred route in Silicon Valley. Bank loans have not
been right for capital-intensive, high-growth ventures because
the ventures mostly do not have positive cash flow, nor do the
entrepreneurs want to offer personal guarantees or the collateral
demanded by the banks.

In Silicon Valley, most billion-dollar entrepreneurs delayed VC
until after they had evidence of the venture's growth potential *and*
the entrepreneur's leadership potential. By doing so, they stayed
on as CEO and were not replaced by a professional executive.

Outside Silicon Valley, most billion-dollar entrepreneurs did not
use VC. They used their savings along with money from family,
friends, and angels. Most of them continued growing without

VC. About 10 percent got VC after VCs could see evidence of venture and leadership potential. By doing so, entrepreneurs stayed in control and remained as CEO. To grow without VC, these entrepreneurs channeled the limited amount of funds that they could raise.

Why Channel?

There are many reasons for using capital-efficient principles—at least till Aha, when potential is evident. Billion-dollar entrepreneurs who got VC early lost control of their business. The VCs brought in a professional executive. Sometimes it worked, as with eBay. Sometimes it failed, as with Apple.

About 20–40 percent of entrepreneurs are replaced as CEOs by the VCs who fund early and take control, while only six percent of the billion-dollar entrepreneurs got VC early. Founding-entrepreneurs who got VC early lost control of their business and kept less of the wealth created.

As noted earlier, 99.9 percent of entrepreneurs don't get VC and 80 percent of those who do get it end up failing. So, 99.98 percent of US entrepreneurs have a good reason to channel because they will not succeed with VC.

VCs also focus on high-potential ventures in emerging industries. This means that entrepreneurs who are not in these favored industries are unlikely to get VC.

VCs also is more easily available in certain areas such as Silicon Valley. Entrepreneurs outside Silicon Valley have a tougher time getting VC. And if they do get it, they usually get it from second-tier VCs who mostly don't have the track record of building unicorns.

Losses Are Tough to Finance

The accepted wisdom is that startups lose money because they have fixed costs or high expenses at the start and no sales to cover these expenses.

VCs are accustomed to losses in the ventures they finance—even though they mainly fund after Aha. VC-funded ventures often seek to achieve high-growth rates to dominate emerging industries. To do so, these ventures spend money before they have the sales for the higher level of expenses. Growing with losses means that entrepreneurs need additional external financing, which VCs can fund. This additional financing dilutes the entrepreneurs.

But VCs continue funding only as long as the venture is growing and showing its potential to dominate its emerging industry. If the venture does not live up to its promise, VCs may stop investing, which may cause the venture to fail.

The billion-dollar entrepreneurs in my study, for the most part, did not lose money. They did not want to lose their own money and could not, or would not, raise money that they would lose. Their decision was influenced by the difficulty of finding money, the high cost of money at this stage, and the risk of losing control of the venture. If billion-dollar entrepreneurs did lose money, it was a small amount. If they needed to raise funds, they used sources that did not demand control such as friends or family. Or they obtained funding from vendors or alliance partners. These entrepreneurs proved their potential by growing sales, and they made a profit by controlling expenses. Essentially, they developed their skills and used finance-smart strategies to grow without losses and stayed in control by reducing financial needs.

Working Capital Needs Can Be Reduced or Funded by Alternative Sources

Working capital finances inventory, accounts receivable, and other current assets not funded by suppliers, employees, and short-term financiers. Inventory is tough to finance because it can be difficult to liquidate. Receivables may be tough to finance if the customers are weak, or unlikely to pay on time, or unlikely to pay in full if the company fails. In the digital age, there is less need for inventory because many e-ventures sell e-stuff, such as information, not hard products.

To channel their equity, finance-smart entrepreneurs reduced needs by using many strategies such as keeping close tabs on inventory, eliminating accounts receivable, linking their growth rate to their cash flow, and/or by reversing the cash-to-cash cycle. Mostly, they got paid before they had to pay. Amancio Ortega built Zara with a faster supply chain.[12]

Bob Kierlin linked Fastenal's growth rate to the level of inventory and gross margins and was able to grow at 30 percent annually from internal cash flow.[13]

Dick Schulze built Best Buy by getting his suppliers to fund his growth.[14]

Fixed Assets Can Be Funded by Cheaper Money

Fixed assets, which include general purpose real estate and equipment, are the easiest assets to finance, and the cost of such financing is usually much lower than that charged by VCs. This is why most ventures finance their fixed assets through leasing.

Billion-dollar entrepreneurs usually avoid the need for fixed assets by outsourcing any non-proprietary functions that require fixed assets. They lease fixed assets that they absolutely need, and often get their customers to finance them. Or they set up long-term contracts from customers and use this contract to obtain funding. By keeping fixed assets low, billion-dollar entrepreneurs usually keep their break-even levels low, especially in the early years when their sales were minimal.

Bob Kierlin built Fastenal into the largest nuts-and-bolts company in the United States by leasing assets until he could buy them from internal cash flow. Therefore, instead of buying used trucks that often broke down, Kierlin bought new trucks in large quantities directly from the manufacturer at attractive prices. After using them for a year, the company sold these trucks at retail for approximately the same price that it had paid for them.

Finding Growth while Saving Scarce Equity

Until the venture's potential is proven and you become an attractive prospect to financiers, you need to grow with limited capital. To position your business for growth and dominance in an attractive market, find ways to grow for less, especially when money is scarce and expensive.

Billion-dollar entrepreneurs grow for less by channeling their scarce equity to smart marketing strategies such as public relations. Since journalists want to write about exciting ventures, your venture may be able to get free publicity, which can also be more effective in getting sales and resources than spending heavily on paid advertising.

Bill Gates is supposed to have said that if he was down to his last dollar, he would spend it on public relations.[15] Gates found it easier to get free publicity because he was dominating a very attractive, emerging market. And his youth and entrepreneurial success made it easier for him to get publicity. Less exciting ventures may not get as much attention. Publicity is attractive for entrepreneurs because it is usually not as expensive as paid advertising, and most importantly, it is more credible. Most customers have been conditioned to not take advertising very seriously, but they respond more favorably to the comments of reputable media or influencers.

Conclusion

Unlike VC-funded ventures that seek lots of cash, billion-dollar entrepreneurs grow with positive cash flow and do not have to raise VC to fund negative cash flow. They do not waste scarce equity to push the market faster than its natural speed or spend massive amounts on marketing. Instead, they reduce their losses and their needs for working capital by adjusting their business and finance strategies and by finding capital-efficient methods to grow without spending lots of capital. In addition, they channel their scarce equity to areas that cannot be financed through alternate methods.

Chapter 8

Use Alt-VC First

US entrepreneurs have many choices for funding. In addition to debt and government-based development finance sources, US entrepreneurs can select from many equity sources. Silicon Valley VCs are the best known of these, but the best equity sources for most entrepreneurs may be Alt-VC sources, especially outside of Silicon Valley.

The US financial system is complex, but it is one of the world's best in its ability to fund entrepreneurs. To paraphrase an old Sinatra song, if you cannot find money here, you will have a tough time everywhere.

Corporate CFOs use investment bankers to help them find the right financing. Entrepreneurs need to figure out how to navigate the complex financing world on their own.[iii] Knowing the US financial system, the best sources, the right instruments, and the factors that affect financing, can help you find the right financing.

---

iii   For more on venture financing, see "Finance Any Business Intelligently" and "Handbook of Business Finance"; www.uEntrepreneurs.com

Factors that Affect Financing

The following factors can affect your financing.

STAGE: The stage of your venture could be the most important factor affecting the financing you get. At high-risk early stages, it is difficult to get VC funding from institutional financiers. At this stage, the most likely sources are noninstitutional equity sources, collateral-based debt, and government-sponsored financing. As the business grows and risk is reduced, more financial options are available.

AMOUNT: It helps to know the amount of financing you need, when you need it, what you need it for, and how much you should get from debt, equity, and development finance. Your business should secure the right amount to achieve its goals. Entrepreneurs often get less than they need because it is difficult and expensive to obtain funding for newer or riskier businesses; and forecasting accurately for startups is difficult. But without the right amount, the business could fail. The right amount depends on factors such as sales goals, assets needed, profitability, cash flow, and the length of time for which financing is raised. The business also needs to find the right amount by use. The uses for the funds can include operating expenses (this usually means losses), inventory, accounts receivable, equipment, and real estate. Some uses, such as fixed assets, are usually easier to finance than others. In addition to the uncertainty about the amount needed, it is also difficult to predict how much you can raise. This is especially true for equity. Seek financing for the scenario that fits your goals and opportunity and is based on market conditions but have alternate scenarios if your first plan fails.

SOURCES: The right sources are those that fit the company's needs today and in the future and which offer the flexibility to adjust as the business's situation changes. The US has one of the most sophisticated financial systems in the world; there is a type of institution for each type of need and, in some cases, many different types of institutions for each type of need. In general, these institutions can be classified as lenders, lessors, equity sources, and development financiers. Additionally, there are many types of institutions within each of these categories. Using the right sources can help your business reach its goals, have a more efficient financing process, and reduce costs. Factors that influence sources include:

- 💰 Proof of potential: Proven ventures usually find it easier to obtain the desired kinds of financing than unproven ones.

- 💰 Level of potential: The higher the proven potential, the more attractive you are to investors. Usually, professional investors seek ventures that can dominate high-potential, emerging industries or niche markets.

- 💰 Cash flow and collateral: Lenders and lessors are more attracted to businesses that have cash flow and collateral.16

BEST COMBINATION: The right financing for a business includes the right combination of financing sources, instruments, and structure. Raising the right financing for a new, emerging, or mid-sized business is challenging. Most entrepreneurs are unaware that banks and VCs are not the only financing sources available to them. Also, most financial advisors have expertise in a few areas of venture financing and tend to focus on these types of financing. Some advisors also avoid startups because of the extra work, the higher risk in the venture, and more uncertainty in the fund-raising process.

ALTERNATE EQUITY SOURCES: Alt-VC sources can include:

- 💰 Entrepreneur's savings: Other investors are always impressed when a young entrepreneur has been able to save a nest-egg, however small, and is willing to invest it in the venture. It shows frugality and commitment. Dick Schulze started with nine thousand dollars of his own savings. He earned this money initially as a teenager fixing his friends' car radios, and then he became a sales rep for Sony after graduating from high school. This was the start of Best Buy.

💰 Friends and family are often the next source of equity: Some entrepreneurs have been fortunate enough to have friends and family who can invest significant sums of capital. Sam Walton started with $25,000 from his wife's family. Bob Kierlin started Fastenal with $31,000 from his own savings and investments from friends. Jeff Bezos got funding from his family to start Amazon.com. So did Mark Zuckerberg for Facebook.

💰 Angels including crowd-funders and angel groups: The promotion of the need for alternate early-stage financing has led to the formation of numerous angel groups and crowdfunding organizations in the US and around the world. Most angels and crowd-funders are interested in helping their area while hitting the jackpot. Crowd-funders usually invest smaller amounts than angels, and the most successful crowdfunding projects have been those funded by potential consumers of the product being developed. Oculus Rift was funded by crowd-funders, and companies like Apple secured funding from angels before the VCs swooped in.

💰 Business alliances such as customers and vendors and corporations seeking technologies: Alliances have usually been the favored institutional source of funding for most entrepreneurs, just as friends, family and angels have been the favored noninstitutional source. One of the most famous users of alliance funding was Michael Bloomberg who got funding from Merrill Lynch to start his namesake company. Others who used alliances included UnitedHealthcare and Chipotle. Richard Burke got funding from physician groups to start UnitedHealthcare. Steve Ells got funding from McDonald's to grow Chipotle. Business alliances are attractive not just for the money. Entrepreneurs also often get a customer, supplier, or growth expertise. And the terms are usually not as onerous as those from venture capitalists.

💰 Alt-VC funds that do not demand control: There are many kinds of VCs. They can range from VCs who finance entrepreneurs in depressed areas or in certain geographic areas such as particular states. Other VCs, also called small-business investment companies, do not seek control of the venture, but they usually invest in the growth stage and in instruments that are less risky to them and less dilutive to the entrepreneur. FedEx was financed by small-business investment companies. Supercomputer manufacturer Cray Research was financed by small-business investment companies and by a community-development corporation focused on low-income areas.

Start with Family and Friends

Family and friends are the kinds of angels who invest in your business because of the relationship. They usually take the most risks. Most entrepreneurs who do not come from wealthy families are limited in the amounts they can raise from these connections. The problem with using friends and family and losing their money is that you may not be able to go home for Thanksgiving. But for many, there are no sources of funding at the earliest stage other than friends and family. Michael Dell started with money from his family. That is how he kept control of his company and used funding from his customers and credit from his suppliers to build a giant company.

Jeff Bezos and Mark Zuckerberg also used family money to start their business. Then, they got angel funding, and finally VCs when they could retain control of their business.

The next round of funding after family and friends often includes angels and other "sophisticated" financiers. These sources often provide greater amounts of funding than family and friends.

Chapter 9

Grow with Angels You Control

Angel financing are a great source of funding for nearly all ventures—if you can get it. The key is to use a group of angel investors. That way, you won't lose control after getting all your funding from just one. This means you have to let go of the "easy" money that may be dangled in front of you and can look at the long-term gain by taking less and keeping control of your venture.

Some entrepreneurs hope that they can build a big new business by following these steps:

- 💰   Get a brilliant idea.
- 💰   Write a business plan.
- 💰   Get initial funding from friends and family.
- 💰   Search for angels (individual professional investors).
- 💰   Contact VCs to attract the first round of VC.
- 💰   Seek more rounds of VC financing to fund losses.
- 💰   Attract investment bankers for an IPO.

💰 Become a billionaire.

Your chances of succeeding with the above strategy may be the same as your odds of winning the lottery. Angels may act as stepping-stones to VC and an IPO. Estimates are that it works about fifteen to sixty times per year and, as noted before, mainly in Silicon Valley when high-potential industries are emerging. But for most, angel financing can be the limiting factor.

Types of Angels

Types of angels include the following:

1. Industry angels such as executives or experts in your industry who often invest significant amounts of money due to their corporate positions or past successes. They can also have attractive industry connections, add credibility to the venture, and open key doors. They are usually the best angels.

2. Area angels invest to build local businesses. They can be desirable if they have experience in building businesses, as many of the Silicon Valley angels do.

3. Rich investors are usually known to local money managers or investment bankers. To reach them, entrepreneurs may have to hire an investment banker. But investment bankers often stay away from new, unproven concepts due to the high risk.

4. Crowdfunding is the latest wrinkle in angel finance (covered later).

Factors Affecting Angel Financing

SOME CAVEATS ABOUT ANGELS: Before contacting angels, including friends and family, find a good lawyer. This means someone who knows securities law and its minefield of rules and regulations, including the number of angels you can use, how much money you can raise, etc. The trouble with seeking angels is that the inexperienced ones with smaller amounts for funding may talk to you, but the experienced ones with more money to fund stay hidden because they have gone down this path before and have often lost money (except, perhaps, in Silicon Valley, where all paths seem to lead to a pot of gold). One way to get angels is to get a bell cow, an angel who is well-known, has a good reputation, and has made money. Can you find a lead investor who knows you, knows the industry, is willing to invest, and can attract other investors?

ANGEL CAPITAL IS LIMITED CAPITAL: Most angels invest smaller amounts in earlier stages than institutional VCs and take more risks. They may be tough to find. Compared with the millions of dollars that large VC funds invest, most angels invest in the tens of thousands. However, many angels join angel groups and pool their resources to offer larger amounts. The Angel Capital Association notes that the median amount of funding per angel group per round was $347,000, and this amount can be leveraged by angel groups joining with others to raise significantly larger amounts.[17] The average seed-stage funding from angels was said to be about one million dollars. In comparison, the average VC investment was five million dollars in the early stage.[18]

Angel money can help a venture reach the next level, when VCs may show interest. But angels invest in significantly more ventures than VCs and in earlier stages. This number was estimated at about 67,000 ventures in 2012,[19] which is supposed to be about 21 percent of entrepreneurs who sought angel funding. With only about five thousand VC-funded ventures each year, about 90 percent on average of angel-funded ventures will not get VC.

Perhaps due to the early stage of the investment, the lack of history, or their own expertise in the industries they invest in, angels are mainly instinctive investors. Angels Den, an angel network in the UK, estimates that 73 percent of angels invest based on their gut feeling.[20] Whether instinct is better than the due diligence conducted by VCs is debatable. Both angels and VCs lose on a huge portion of their investments. What separates winners from losers is that winners invest in one or two homeruns out of about 100 investments and own a large stake in these home runs. They find these home runs mainly in Silicon Valley.

IMPLICATIONS: If the strategy is capital intensive, entrepreneurs need to use angel financing to reach Aha, at which point VCs may show an interest. If a capital-intensive venture does not reach Aha, or if the venture cannot find VC, it is likely to fail. Entrepreneurs should design the venture to grow to self-sufficiency with the amount of angel financing that they can raise, instead of gambling on the hope that more money will be available from VCs when they need it. The strategy may be smart in Silicon Valley and if direct competitors have VC. Otherwise, it may end up being just that—a gamble.

ANGELS DO WELL IN SILICON VALLEY: When you read about angels, you will usually hear about their success in Silicon Valley. That is not a coincidence. Angels usually invest locally. Most homeruns are in Silicon Valley, so it does seem logical that many successful angels are located there.

Mark Zuckerberg started Facebook when he was a student at Harvard. Facebook grew very quickly while he was still a student, but his financing came from Silicon Valley angel Peter Thiel who was a cofounder of PayPal. Zuckerberg moved to Silicon Valley, got $500,000 from a group of angels, including Thiel, and kept control. Facebook continued to soar, after which Zuckerberg was able to get VC. [21]

Are there successful angels everywhere, waiting for you to find them? A study of 539 US and UK angels found that angel returns were as attractive as VCs. [22] The study notes that *"these angel investors (across the US and UK) produced a gross multiple of 2.5x their investment, in a mean time of about four years."* This translates to an annual return of about 26 percent, which is phenomenal given that the VC median has been hovering much below that number in the recent past. This result could be due to a small sample of the top angels out of the 300,000 angels in the US (as of June 2018), [23] or it could be a sample of their best investments, or it could be selective memory, or this study may have found truly great angels. But even in this study, *"90 percent of all the cash returns are produced by 10 percent of the exits"* and about 55 percent are said to lose money. Other studies show that most angels do not make money but want to make a difference. [24]

It might be useful to get the perspective of Andy Rachleff, a cofounder of Benchmark Partners, one of the premier VC funds in Silicon Valley, who notes the following: [25]

- 💰 According to Cambridge Associates, twenty VC firms—or 3 percent—make about 95 percent of VC profits.

- 💰 The top VC firms rely on angels to take the initial risk to keep their own returns high.

- 💰 Since most VCs make poor returns and seed rounds are at higher risk, angel returns must be "atrocious."

💰   Ron Conway, a noted Silicon Valley angel, funded
Google through his second fund. This fund did not make
any money.

IMPLICATIONS: Silicon Valley seems to be heaven for angels.
One reason could be that many angels there were successful
entrepreneurs or were team members in growth ventures, so
they know how to build giant companies and give sound advice.
Thiel built PayPal along with Elon Musk and sold it to eBay. He
then funded Facebook. The second reason could be that Silicon
Valley angels are investing in an area that has built one of the
greatest collections of billion-dollar companies the world has
ever seen. Will their skills work outside Silicon Valley? The track
record outside, as measured by billion-dollar ventures, is not as
noteworthy as the one in Silicon Valley.

Even Angels Want an Exit

All angels, including friends and family, want their money back,
hopefully, with an attractive return. For investors to get a nice
return, the venture needs an attractive exit. For an attractive exit,
ventures need to show the potential to dominate in a high-growth
trend. Usually, when the stock markets are not frothy and initial
public offerings (IPOs) are not attractive, high-potential ventures
need multiple rounds of VC funding after the angel round.
Without these additional rounds, the capital-intensive ventures
may not have the staying power and track record for high IPO
valuations. Most Silicon Valley billion-dollar ventures such as
Facebook had multiple rounds of VC funding before going public.

Capital-intensive ventures that do not get additional rounds of
equity financing may fail. To survive, these ventures may need
to switch to a capital-efficient strategy. But once the venture has
started using a capital-intensive strategy, it is usually difficult
to cut back and return to capital efficiency while keeping
momentum and dominance. A turnaround requires different

skills. Many entrepreneurs who seek to grow with hopes of increasing amounts of VC may not be right for growth without capital. In the meantime, other ventures may have surpassed yours, and it becomes difficult to catch up.

IMPLICATIONS: Think about your exit before raising money. With angel financing, you can choose capital efficiency, or you can gamble with capital intensity. With capital efficiency, you can seek VC for competitive advantage after "Aha," or grow with capital efficiency. When you are growing with self-sufficiency and not desperate for financing, there are likely to be attractive ways for investors to exit. Without capital efficiency, you are gambling that you can get VC before you run out of money. Capital efficiency may give your angels a nice exit.

Bill Gates is a poster child for this strategy. He was growing with capital efficiency. He got venture capital more as a source of advice than money. He had no problems with an exit. Jan Koum built WhatsApp with limited capital from angels who were recruited by his partner. He built WhatsApp to more than 300 million customers with this capital. The VCs were knocking in his door, not the other way around. He took funding from one of them, and they all profited handsomely when Facebook bought WhatsApp for nearly $20 billion.

Angels Can Sometimes Become Sharks

Google had many angels. One was Ram Shriram. Shriram was an executive at Netscape when he left to start Junglee.com. He sold Junglee to Amazon.com and became an executive at Amazon. That is the kind of angel you want—someone who has the track record, the proven skills, and the network to help you grow. Shriram was one of the angels who invested about $250,000 each in Google when it was starting. He netted more than a billion dollars.

But not all angels are created alike. Some can be sharks. Once they get control of a venture, benefits from the venture are likely to flow to them and to their families. Stay in control and find the right angels.

IMPLICATIONS: Each angel has different expectations and demands. Family and friends are more lenient and usually forgiving. But sometimes, entrepreneurs may have to find a new group of family and friends if they lose money (every dollar has its price). Professional investors may bring more experience and expertise. But while they can demand influence, control, or a higher share of the venture causing more dilution to the entrepreneurs, professional investors may also bring deeper pockets and financial connections. Industry executives can be the most helpful since they add credibility and connections and may offer better advice.

Grow with the Crowd

The new strategy to find angels is called crowdfunding, which is emerging due to new legislation that has made it easier for entrepreneurs to obtain funding from investors who give money in smaller amounts. Crowdfunding gets you money in small increments from many different investors who usually find you through an online crowdfunding site. Often, these investors like your product or proposal, want to buy it, or are willing to take a small risk on you. Successful VCs point to their track record to show that they know how to pick winners. Therefore, it is great to see that crowdfunding has its first billion-dollar baby.[26]

Ocular Rift was funded by crowds and sold to Facebook for a few billion. Based on this great achievement from the entrepreneur's perspective since the investors did not share in the goodies, will crowdfunding succeed in the long-term?

Crowdfunding is supposed to be earlier-stage VC with funding from the average investor. It is only the latest in a long line of equity-funding strategies that has been promoted or allowed by the government under the assumption that a shortage of risk capital is blocking the world's entrepreneurial forces from being unleashed. The common pitch is that crowdfunding is VC for those who otherwise cannot get institutional VC. The successes such as Oculus Rift will be trumpeted.[27]

But will crowdfunding be the panacea that many hope for? Crowdfunding is usually done at earlier stages than VC. Earlier stages are riskier stages. Therefore, there will be more losses at earlier stages, and many investors will lose money. A few winners will get a lot of publicity, encouraging more crowd-funders to start financing. But soon, the laws of gravity will cause the inevitable shakeout.

Crowdfunding has many promoters and few gatekeepers. The SEC is supposed to track and monitor. But the SEC cannot gauge quality. No one can read a business plan and predict success. That's why 80 percent of VC-funded ventures fail—and why VC investments are made after Aha! The problem lies in separating the hucksters and failures from the visionaries and the competent. This is impossible and will inevitably lead to a surplus of bad deals and crashes. Crowdfunding is likely to have one-sided financing agreements. When the venture promoters develop the agreements, there is no sophisticated party, like a VC, on the other side who can bring some balance to the table. It will be the entrepreneurs, their lawyers, and the crowdfunding site. Let's hope that the crowdfunding sites can do a reasonable job.

Crowdfunding may get some interest in the short run as an investment vehicle. But will it be a long-term success?

Crowdfunding that is based on pre-sales of products or services is an attractive strategy to get the venture started, as long as the entrepreneur has the capacity to develop the product promised.

But crowdfunding as a financing strategy has some hurdles. Crowdfunding may survive if those who control it understand human psychology. The fact that most gamblers lose money and the fact that most lottery ticket buyers don't win has not stopped the masses from making casinos richer or buying lottery tickets. Also to consider is the fun factor and the excitement that you, too, could be a winner. I think crowdfunding will be similar. Most will lose money, but the few winners will keep the excitement going. The initial honeymoon will fade. But is the marriage strong enough to sustain crowdfunding? Do the crowdfunding players understand that at least a few have to win, and their stories have to be promoted? If every crowd-funder fails in some way, especially when the ventures they fund succeed, say sayonara to crowdfunding.

Use Crowd (and Angel) Capital as if You Will Not Get VC

Nearly all VC is provided after Aha—after the venture shows signs of potential. To reach Aha, you may have to use angel and crowd capital. At Aha, you have more choices.

Since more than half of crowd funded ventures fail, and those that succeed do so "by a little,"[28] entrepreneurs need to make efficient use of the limited capital they get.

Entrepreneurs who get crowd capital and angel capital (CC/AC) may assume that they will get VC, and therefore develop a capital-intensive strategy. As noted earlier, very few of those getting CC/AC will get VC.

Most of the ventures that get CC/AC do not get VC. Here are some reasons:

- 💰 Failure: Obviously, the risk of failure is high in new ventures.

- 💰 Lack of potential: VCs like to invest in ventures with proof of high potential and high growth. Many of the ventures funded by angels may not have the potential to become big.

- 💰 Unattractive industry: VCs focus on emerging, high-potential industries.

- 💰 Unattractive location: Most of the successful VCs are in Silicon Valley, and most of their successful investments are in Silicon Valley. If you are outside Silicon Valley, you may not attract VC.

- 💰 Inability to dominate an emerging industry: VCs like ventures that can dominate.

The best reason for not choosing not to get VC is because you don't need VC and your venture can grow without it. Billion-dollar entrepreneurs who grew to more than a billion dollars in sales and valuation without VC include Chipotle (Steve Ells), Dell (Michael Dell), and Under Armour (Kevin Plank). Some entrepreneurs don't seek VC because they cannot accept investors' terms, including dilution and loss of control. So, they learn to grow without VC.

What should you do? You should assume that the CC/AC you get is all the capital you will get and adjust the business to grow without additional outside capital. If you can continue to grow without VC, you can control the venture and reduce dilution, then assess competitors. If your direct competitors have VC, you may need it. Billion-dollar entrepreneurs chose to seek VC when they learned their competitors had VC.

If your venture is *not* one that is likely to get VC, you need to grow with the limited funds you raise or borrow until you attract alternate sources that allow you to grow on your terms. And if your venture is one that *could* attract VCs, you need to reach Aha with the limited funds you have raised and not run out of cash.

Chapter 10

Seek Non-VC VCs First

There are alternate sources of equity. Most of them offer significant amounts and may not seek control. Seek them.

Seek Alliances

An attractive source of equity funding is corporate alliances. Many billion-dollar entrepreneurs grow with alliances.

This source can be very attractive when used right. Corporations have money and clout. They are connected and can open many doors. However, they may want options to acquire your company after it is proven. Unless you negotiate a smart deal, the upside may be limited.

One of the greatest alliances of all time—from the perspective of the entrepreneur—is the one between Microsoft and IBM. IBM paid Microsoft a fee for the use of the operating system acquired by Microsoft. By allowing Microsoft to license the operating system to other companies, IBM enabled it to become the standard of the PC industry—with Microsoft in firm control.[29]

Alliances can also be used to develop a new product. Finding support from deep-pocket alliance partners who can gain strategically can be advantageous due to two factors: garnering the first customer and getting money at lower cost than money attained from VCs. Done right, alliances can be a very attractive source of funding.

Mike Bloomberg used his alliance with Merrill Lynch to build Bloomberg and amass one of the world's biggest fortunes. Merrill Lynch originally invested $30 million in Bloomberg in return for 30 percent of the company.[30] Merrill also benefited from Bloomberg's product. Mike Bloomberg not only got the funding he needed but also a major client and credibility—and he kept control of the company.

Alliances can also be used to help large corporations enter emerging trends where they have no experience. Richard Burke used corporate alliances to build UnitedHealth. Burke found the initial seed capital for his company from Charter Medical Corporation, a psychiatric hospital chain in Macon, Georgia. Charter Medical's employees staffed the HMO for a percentage of the HMO's gross revenues. After selling his interest in the alliance to Charter, Burke formed alliances with physician groups to form HMOs. The doctors were often skeptical, but knew they needed to do something different because of the potential loss of their patients to group practice or to staff-model HMOs under the new federal HMO-enabling legislation. The doctors typically did not want to invest money up front to develop a business plan, organize the HMO and/or obtain the needed approvals to operate. Burke's new company performed these tasks for them, thus minimizing the upfront investment required from the sponsoring physicians. Since Burke was absorbing all the upfront cost and risk, he insisted on very long-term management contracts to recoup his investment and earn an attractive return.

When Burke had enough HMOs under contract, he went public and bought out the physicians' interest.

Alliances can also be organized with customers and suppliers who have a vested interest. Dick Schulze used extended terms from suppliers such as Sony and Panasonic to finance Best Buy.

Brett Shockley of Spanlink and Rod Burwell of Xerxes Corporation got advances from their customers, which they used to build hundred-million-dollar companies.

But there are pitfalls with alliances:

- 💰 Some corporate partners want to absorb the technology from ventures, after which they won't support the venture. Make sure you protect your interests.

- 💰 Corporations often seek a right of first refusal to buy your company when you are ready to exit. Having this clause in your financing agreement could be a hindrance since you may not get attractive offers from potential strategic acquirers when you are ready to exit.

Find Alt-VC Venture Capitalists

Sometimes entrepreneurs may be forced to get venture capital, such as when a direct competitor with the same business model is able to raise more capital and you have nothing to beat them with other than money. Michael Dell had direct competitors with VC, but he was able to use his direct-to-consumer model to succeed without VC. On the other hand, Pierre Omidyar of eBay succeeded with internal cash flow when he attracted direct competitors using the same business model, but with more capital. He was forced to seek VC. But even when this happens, entrepreneurs who know alternate sources of venture capital can do better than those using the traditional VC route. Even within the VC world, there are ways to get VC without losing control.

Corporate VCs (CVC)

Corporations fund ventures directly via alliances or by using their own VC funds. CVCs can be attractive since their terms are often financially less onerous than early-stage VC limited partnerships, and they can invest large amounts of money. They also bring credibility to a venture and often invest in very early stages, such as at the research and development stage when early-stage VC limited partnerships may be hesitant. However, as noted earlier, they can often seek the right of first refusal to buy the venture, which could reduce exit values, or they may seek access to the technology.

When Earl Bakken started Medtronic, his first pacemaker had an external battery. When the Chardack-Greatbatch battery was introduced, Bakken formed an alliance, licensed it, and developed the first internal cardiac pacemaker. Allying with the developer of the battery helped Medtronic become the dominant medical electronics company. And the company has followed a similar strategy since then to find new and unique medical technologies that it can fund and use as vehicles for further growth. Toward this end, Medtronic has been active as a VC to fund new entrepreneurs.

Late-Stage VCs

Late-stage VCs may not require, as the early-stage VCs do, that the founder-entrepreneur be replaced as CEO by a corporate executive. This reduces dilution and allows the entrepreneur to retain control of the business. About 18 percent of billion-dollar entrepreneurs, including Gates and Bezos, built their companies with late-stage equity. But you need to reach this stage without VC.

Mark Zuckerberg took this one step further and demanded voting proxies from his investors. So instead of operating with the VC in control, Zuckerberg retained firm command of his venture. The founders of Google (Alphabet) and Snap also demanded control.

Small-Business Investment Companies (SBIC)

SBICs are licensees of the federal government. SBICs were one of the first organized institutional VC funds, and they were formed to offer more equity funding to US ventures.

SBICs use their investors' funds, leveraged with debt from the federal government, to invest in businesses. Due to their own debt service needs, SBICs usually finance later-stage businesses that are expected to have the cash flow needed to pay debt service. Most of them are similar to mezzanine funds in their financing practices. The exception to the above are SBICs that are owned by banks. These SBICs often behave like early-stage VCs.

Billion-dollar entrepreneurs, such as Fred Smith of Fedex and Elon Musk of Tesla, received funding from SBICs.[31]

The shortcomings of SBICs encouraged legislation that allowed pension funds to invest in VC limited partnerships, which gave rise to the current-day VC industry. One of the principal shortcomings of SBICs was the use of leverage to enhance the size of the VC fund. This meant that the SBICs themselves borrowed money from the Small Business Administration (SBA) that they had to repay. Borrowing money to invest in high-risk ventures is not a sound financial policy, so SBICs mainly fund later-stage ventures after most of the risk has been reduced. Another shortcoming was the short life span of the loan, which forced the SBIC to finance at later stages in ventures that had positive cash flow or which could get it soon.

Area & Community Venture Capital Funds

Area VC funds are a good source for entrepreneurs, especially since they are interested in local deals. Reach out to local VCs before contacting the national Silicon Valley VCs. After your local angels, your chances of getting equity may be better with your local VCs than with VCs in Silicon Valley or around the country.

If your business is in an inner-city area or in an economically depressed area, or if you are willing to relocate there, consider a community-development VC fund, or a community-development financial institution (CDFI). These institutions do not exist everywhere, but they can be an attractive source where they exist. Contact your local economic-development organization; they may be willing to help find these funds.

Billion-dollar entrepreneurs such as Seymour Cray of Cray Research and Sam Walton of Walmart benefited from CDFI funding.[iv]

Conclusion

Since 99.9 percent of ventures don't get VC, and an additional 80 percent fail with it, knowing the right source for you and your venture could mean the difference between failure, success, and a home run. Knowing the right source could mean the difference between profiting from your venture or others profiting, and whether you run your venture or someone else does.

Again, if VCs are not interested in your venture due to your early stage, bring your venture to Aha by being capital efficient. At that stage, you may find that you can grow without VC if you are outside Silicon Valley and with control if you are in Silicon Valley.

---

iv   The author funded these two companies when he was vice-president of a financial institution.

Entrepreneurs such as Mark Zuckerberg delayed getting VC until Aha. At takeoff, he could dictate terms. Same with WhatsApp. To do this, you need to find alternate sources of funding, including:

- 💰 Smarter (for you) sources such as friends, family, angels, corporate alliance partners, and crowdfunding.

- 💰 Scalable-debt sources that need proof of repayment capacity.

- 💰 Development financiers who offer lower-cost funding.

- 💰 Internal funding by being finance smart and adjusting your strategy for capital efficiency.

- 💰 Finance-smart strategies to grow more with less.

Chapter 11

Seek Scalable Debt

Some types of debt such as amortizing loans can limit your growth because of the need to reduce principal. Other types of loans can grow with your business because they are automatically refinanced as asset levels increase. Seek the kinds of loans that can grow with your assets to avoid constraining your business.

The typical high-growth venture in Silicon Valley does not use debt because:

- 💰 Debt needs to be repaid and is mostly repaid from cash flow. Most Silicon Valley ventures are seeking to grow and dominate their emerging industries by reinvesting their cash flow and any additional cash they can raise. Their focus is on domination, not on positive cash flow.

- 💰 Lenders are usually not interested in funding businesses with negative cash flow.

- 💰 Many commonly used debt instruments are structured as amortizing loans where the principal is repaid in installments. This can reduce the amount of capital that is left over for use by the company and can restrict growth.

Types of Scalable Debt

Many billion-dollar and hundred-million-dollar entrepreneurs have built great companies by using debt—judiciously. Here are some of the ways they do this.

Line of Credit

A line of credit is usually obtained from a bank. A line offers a flexible financing sources by allowing the business to continuously borrow based on asset levels, and repay so long as the loan is within its limits and the business meets loan covenants.

Joel Ronning of Digital River used a line of credit in his second venture. He built this venture to $40 million in sales with a $40,000 investment, and this investment was also borrowed via a credit card. To grow with limited cash, he sold direct to consumers, got paid before he had to pay his vendors, and tightly controlled his expenses.

Harold Roitenberg built Modern Merchandising into a six billion dollars (sales) company by selling franchises to entrepreneurs. Roitenberg got trade credit from vendors based on the financial strength of his franchisees. Then he got a printer to print the catalog on credit. He sold the catalog to his franchisees. As the franchisees paid for the catalog, he paid the printer. With no investment, he built the company to about twenty million dollars in sales, most of which was profit. He used these profits to start buying his franchisees, went public, and bought many of the other franchisees.

Transaction Loan

Transaction loans are made for a single purpose and the loan is repaid when the purpose is accomplished. It is usually a short-term loan and relies on the collateral to be liquidated or on the cash flow expected from the project or from refinancing.

Gary Holmes built a real-estate empire valued in the hundreds of millions by funding all his projects separately. Holmes had equity partners for each project. He optioned the land, developed the plans, and signed leases with anchor tenants, including Best Buy. With the assets and leases, he obtained debt to build and launch the project.

Leases

A lease can be an attractive alternative to a loan in order to finance fixed assets, i.e. equipment and real estate. Leases can be operational (i.e. shorter term) or financial (i.e. longer-term, which usually amortize the cost of the asset). Leasing can help you expand faster and improve cash flow, especially if you don't have to put any money down as you would with an equipment loan.

Dick Schulze built Best Buy by leasing the needed real estate and equipment. He did not invest any of his scarce cash in fixed assets at the start. But he had to make sure that the cash flow from his stores was sufficient to pay the leases on time.

Sam Walton of Walmart did the same when he was building his chain around the US. One of his appointed developers would buy the land, get Walmart as the anchor, and lease space to smaller stores. The developer financed the real estate using market sources, and Walmart expanded without a down payment for the real estate.

Glenn Hasse built Ryt-Way into a $100 million+ food packager by offering great service to his large food-company customers. When he needed equipment to process an order, Hasse asked the customer to fund the equipment.

Trade Credit

Trade credit is usually the "cheapest" form of financing. The cost is usually built into the price of the products or services you purchase. Try to establish credit with your suppliers by sharing data about your business so they give you credit. This could dramatically reduce your financing needs and your cost of financing. Also ask for extended terms when you become an important customer.

Dick Schulze got trade credit with extended terms for his inventory. By making sure that he paid his suppliers on time, he was able to build Best Buy into a giant.

When Sam Walton realized that he was buying more from large companies such as P&G than they were selling in the entire country of Japan, he asked these companies to open offices in Bentonville, Arkansas, where Walmart is headquartered. He then cut out all intermediaries and asked for favored pricing.

Amazon.com did the same, initially in the book business and subsequently in the other businesses Bezos entered. He got extended terms from his suppliers, including book sellers. However, he collected cash from his customers and benefited from the float by delaying payment to his vendors.

Customer Advances

Developing a business model where the customers pay in advance can offer working capital for "unlimited" growth, especially if this advance is combined with trade credit. This can be done when you are selling direct to consumers, which has been made easier in the Internet age.

Michael Dell built Dell by selling direct to consumers. He did this before the age of the Internet. By selling directly to consumers, Dell got their cash in advance. Customers were willing to do this and pay full price because Dell allowed them to buy a customized PC and get the latest technology. And he used their cash to grow.

Brett Shockley of Spanlink developed the automated telephone answering systems that connected the customer's phone number with their database. He customized this service for his business customers and asked customers to make advance payments. He used this money for working capital.

Rod Burwell built Xerxes into a $400 million+ business starting with plastic barge covers. He asked his large corporate customers, such as Cargill, to pay in advance, which they did because of the product's advantages.

Jill Blashack Strahan of Tastefully Simple built a $140 million+ company with ownership of about 70 percent and an investment of around $35,000. She had her customers pay for her gourmet foods before she had to pay her vendors.

Getting advances and cash payments from customers are among the best sources of funding for entrepreneurs because they are part of the value-adding chain. Consumers are used to paying when they receive a product or service, often in advance and on a monthly basis as the online subscription services sellers are realizing. But this means that you may need to adjust your business model.

Sources for Scalable Debt

Financial institutions that help you obtain scalable debt include the following:

Asset-Based Lenders

Asset-based lenders are mainly working capital and short-term lenders. They usually offer highly monitored working capital loans with inventory and receivables as collateral, and are often called in when a bank feels uncomfortable with a loan, such as in a turnaround situation. But asset-based lenders usually charge a much higher interest rate to offset the risk in your business and their higher cost of monitoring. Use asset-based lenders for their flexible financing ability and have your bank participate in the loan to reduce your cost.

Commercial Banks

Commercial banks are the supermarket for debt. They offer all types of financial services, but they don't like risk. While commercial banks want a history of cash flow, they may be willing to offer loans, such as revolving lines of credit, if you have strong accounts receivable and if they get can government guarantees. Bank financing is often one of the best financing sources for entrepreneurs who are not good candidates to receive financing from angels and VCs. It is relatively cheap when the interest rate and dilution is compared with the cost and covenants of angel and VC financing. But about 95 percent of entrepreneurs do not get angel financing, and about 99.9 percent do not get VC financing. On the other hand, banks nearly always demand personal guarantees and collateral, especially for younger and weaker businesses. Bank financing also have lower interest rates than loans from asset-based lenders, but asset-based lenders lend to companies that may have weaker financial statements and performance so long as their accounts receivable are strong. See the earlier note about asset-based lenders.

Sales-Finance Companies

Sales-finance companies are involved in financing consumer loans either directly to consumers or via retailers who originate the loans. Businesses that sell big-ticket items to consumers can usually sell the loan to sales-finance companies. Sales-finance companies are an attractive source of financing because they enable consumers to buy these items, such as cars. Not many people are able to pay cash for these items, so vendors can generate more sales by offering such financing to their customers. In most cases, the business generating the loan also gets a loan origination fee from the sales-finance company, offering another source of revenue. However, businesses that bring in a sales-finance company and sell them the loan should worry about the quality of the customer and the quality of the loan. If the customer defaults on the payment, the lender may have "recourse" to the business, i.e. they may expect the business to buy the loan back.

Leasing Companies

An advantage of leasing, as opposed to purchasing, is that a business can use equipment without a down payment or with a smaller down payment. Rather than locking up money in fixed assets such as real estate or equipment that can more easily be leased at a much lower cost than that for equity, entrepreneurs should be able to use this amount more productively in other parts of the business that are more difficult to finance such as working capital.

Leasing can also be useful when the business does not have the income to make use of depreciation, and can get better rates by passing on these benefits to someone who can. This means that entrepreneurs can get financing for the asset at a lower cost by leasing because the owner of the asset is getting the tax benefits of depreciation, and since newer ventures may not have the high level of profits to take advantage of the tax benefits of ownership. The tax benefits of depreciation can be added to the benefits of a lower financial return and make the total more attractive to lessors.

Billion-dollar entrepreneurs such as Sam Walton (Walmart) and Dick Schulze (Best Buy) leased their fixed assets, including fixtures and real estate. This strategy allowed them to grow faster and dominate their market.

Factoring Companies

Factoring companies buy accounts receivable from businesses. Factors usually assume the risk of collection, which is useful in some types of businesses such as international trade. Some factoring companies resort to "recourse" factoring, where they seek to collect uncollectable accounts receivables from the seller. This form may not be attractive given its high cost. Factoring has had a mixed reputation in American business, with some industries accepting it and others considering it a sign of financial weakness.

Ken Dahlberg of Dahlberg Electronics and Buffalo Wild Wings started in business by placing coin-operated stereos in hospital rooms. After the stereos started generating cash flow, Dahlberg sold the equipment and the income streams to a large hospital vendor. Among the unicorn entrepreneurs I studied or interviewed, he is the only one who obtained financing by selling receivables.

Internet-Based Lending

Increasingly, Internet-based lending is helping stronger, small-midsized businesses obtain funding. The Internet has also developed new types of financing, including crowd-sourcing and P2P (person-to-person) lending, which are competing with banks. Institutions are increasingly entering the P2P space and siphoning off the best deals.[32] P2P lending replaces the financial institution, such as a bank, with the online intermediary acting as a matchmaker between a borrower and the lender. Lenders absorb the default risk of the loan and gets a slightly higher rate than they would get by placing the loan as a deposit at the bank. Borrowers get a lower rate than they would from a bank. The intermediary site collects a small fee.

Examples of P2P lenders are Prosper Marketplace and Lending Club. While the benefits to the business are evident (lower interest rates), it is not clear whether the benefit to the lender (higher rates) is offset by the increased risk of default.

Development Financiers

Many local, state, and federal governments offer financing to help area entrepreneurs and small businesses. These loans are usually below-market-rate financing and have easier financial criteria. Development finance is usually provided by the following:

- 💰 Local governments, foundations, and nonprofit development corporations that offer equity, debt, and grants to businesses that can grow and create jobs. One very attractive source of financing for local manufacturers and other job creators is a program called tax increment financing that allows the business to benefit from the increased property tax paid by the development.

- 💰 All states offer business financing programs ranging from loans, loan guarantees, and venture capital. Some offer tax benefits to investors who offer equity to new ventures. Others act as a conduit for federal money for local development. These programs are often more prevalent in states that are seeking more economic development and in areas that are more economically depressed such as inner cities or low-income rural areas.

💰 The federal government has a variety of programs that offer financing for business development and job creation. The largest of these is the Small Business Administration that offers a variety of loan programs through intermediaries, such as commercial banks and nonprofit development corporations.

Development finance programs are usually cheaper from a financial perspective but have more business or financial criteria since nearly all are targeted to small businesses or designated beneficiaries.

Conclusion

To use scalable debt, you need cash flow to repay interest and principal. This is not always possible in emerging industries. In such a case, grab all the VC you can—if you can get it on reasonable terms. This is what Uber and Airbnb did. But very few are like Uber and Airbnb.

Finance-smart billion-dollar entrepreneurs such as Sam Walton, Dick Schulze, Niraj Jain, Michael Dell, and others used scalable debt from various sources to grow. The key to their use of scalable debt was that they were not handicapped by the use of debt. They could pay the cost of the debt, whether in the form of interest costs, leases, or the cost to the vendor, and repay principal. Often the debt was in the form of short-term credit as in accounts payable or in the form of long-term leases for fixed assets. By doing so, they could grow along with or faster than their direct competitors, and with positive cash flow.

Chapter 12

Choose Smarter Instruments

The US has more diverse financial instruments for venture development than nearly any other country in the world. Use the instruments that help you grow, stay in control, reduce risk for financiers, and reduce dilution for you.

Financial instruments include equity, hybrid, debt, and leasing instruments, and each has its own use, cost, risk, and method of repayment. The right financial instruments can better align entrepreneurs' and financiers' interests to reach agreement.

The types of financial instruments you use and their terms should be matched with the company, the type of asset, cash flow available, risk, payback term, cost, and covenants. Matching correctly can lower the risk and cost of financing.[33]

Equity and Hybrid Instruments

Equity and hybrid instruments include common stock, preferred stock (mainly convertible), convertible debt, warrants, franchising a way to get equity, and employee stock-ownership trusts. Equity and hybrid instruments require a share of the company in the form of immediate ownership or the right to buy shares in the future. These instruments carry the highest risk for investors and are the most expensive for entrepreneurs in terms of dilution and risk of losing control. Their advantage is that they reduce the risk and cost of bankruptcy.

The following instruments can help you finance your business and stay in control; however, some of these instruments can have clauses that give financiers control under certain circumstances.

Non-Controlling Common Shares

This strategy could include sales of a minority share of the company, shares without voting rights, or fewer voting rights than other shares of common stock sold to insiders. In early rounds, non-controlling common shares are often sold to family, friends, small angels, and unsophisticated investors. When sophisticated investors consider common stock, they will usually ask for rights to control and take over the company if the business is in trouble or has not met its goals.

Mark Zuckerberg of Facebook, and Larry Page and Sergey Brin of Google were able to get sophisticated angels to invest significant amounts of funding that still allowed the entrepreneurs to stay in control of the company. Zuckerberg, Page, and Brin stayed in control of their ventures since they had already developed the technology and the momentum in order to dominate an attractive, emerging, high-potential industry.

Preferred Stock

Preferred stock, as used in venture financing, is convertible to common stock and is used along with common stock or subordinated convertible debt to fund new ventures. VC funds normally use preferred stock when making investments since it allows VCs to have a priority over the common shareholders in liquidation and dividends, offers convertibility if there is an upside, and offers clauses to control the venture and protect VC interests that may not be available to common shareholders. They are usually able to get these rights due to their ability to invest larger amounts of funding needed by capital-intensive, high-growth ventures. When used in larger corporations such as utilities, preferred stock is often closer to high-risk bonds in its financial profile, i.e. it offers a dividend but without convertibility to common. Normally, entrepreneurs sell common stock to Alt-VC investors to avoid giving them special rights, but preferred stock may be required when the angels are sophisticated.

Convertibles

A convertible instrument is one that can be converted from one form to another, such as from a loan or preferred stock to common stock. The convertible loan or preferred stock allows investors to have an advantage over common stockholders, while allowing the investors to convert to common when there is an attractive liquidity event. VC limited partnerships usually use convertible preferred stock, while most small-business investment companies (except maybe for bank-owned ones) mainly use convertible debt. Entrepreneurs can use convertible debt to reduce dilution by repaying principal and interest, thereby reducing investors' risk while giving them warrants if there is an upside. The risk is that the ventures may not be able to repay the loan or repurchase the preferred shares when they have to do so and may have to pay a penalty for this inability.

Warrants

A warrant allows the holder to buy a stated number of shares at a designated price for a defined time period. Since it does not obligate the holder to buy the shares, it can be an attractive incentive to investors to take high risks. Warrants are an excellent vehicle for entrepreneurs and for investors. They are usually used as sweeteners with other forms of financing to make the entire package more attractive. As an example, if entrepreneurs want to sell shares for four dollars per share and investors are only willing to pay three dollars, one way to address this issue is to sell the shares at four dollars, but offer warrants along with each share to allow the investor to buy more shares at four dollars for a certain pre-defined time period. By delaying the decision to exercise these warrants, till there is more liquidity in the company's equity, investors get a profit on each warrant without having to risk additional cash buying the warrant. If the venture fails, they don't have to exercise the warrants.

Franchises

Rather than sell shares of the parent company, an expanding company has often sold area franchises to entrepreneurs who want to operate the business in specific areas. Instead of expanding exclusively with company-owned stores or offices, growing ventures can offer their products or services via franchisees. Usually the franchisee is responsible for financing, and pays the franchisor an upfront fee and a royalty based on sales. In addition to leveraging financial resources, franchising also allows a company to leverage managerial resources.

A franchise can be complicated to operate but is a way to get more capital. Billion-dollar entrepreneurs who have built huge businesses on the franchising concept include Ray Kroc, who bought McDonald's when it was a small business in Southern California, and John Schnatter, who founded and built Papa John's Pizza.

Limited Partnerships

Limited partnerships are vehicles that offer investors the upside of equity with the downside limited to their agreed-upon investment. Limited partnerships can be very attractive for certain kinds of businesses such as real-estate development and venture capital. A limited partnership is normally used to raise equity for a business or project, and this is leveraged with debt. The percentage of equity usually ranges from 20 percent to 30 percent of the project's total cost. The main advantages of limited partnerships include:

💰 Limited liability to passive investors

💰 Pass-through of profits and losses, avoiding double-taxation

💰 Subject to certain guidelines, a corporation can be used as a general partner, further limiting personal liability

💰 Profits and losses can be allocated among partners according to prior agreement, allowing the benefits of depreciation and tax credits to be transferred to those who can utilize them

The major disadvantages of limited partnerships include:

💰 Limited partnership interests are not as easily transferred as corporate shares due to a limited secondary market

💰 They may be complex to organize and may require the use of attorneys and accountants

Employee Stock Options Plans (ESOPs)

Many companies have used ESOPs to incentivize their employees with an ownership interest in the business, including companies such as Publix Super Markets and WL Gore and Associates (maker of Gore-Tex). ESOPs also can be attractive as a financing tool due to their tax benefits.

An ESOP is an employee benefit program through which employees can acquire all or part of the stock of the corporation in which they work. A corporation forms an Employee Stock Ownership Trust (ESOT) to purchase its own stock for the benefit of its employees. An ESOT qualifies for favored tax treatment in the Internal Revenue Code. The difference when compared to other pension plans is that an ESOT must invest primarily in employer securities, whereas a pension plan is not allowed to hold large blocks of employer securities.

An ESOT can obtain funds from the parent corporation or borrow funds from financial institutions such as commercial banks or insurance companies. The loans use employer stock as collateral and is repaid by the employer. While there are benefits to employees and the corporation can raise funds, it can result in dilution for existing shareholders. Consider this option if you want your employees to have a share in your company's growth.

Debt and Leasing Instruments

Debt and leasing instruments can range from trade credit to various types of loans and leases. While debt has a lower interest rate than the rate of return expected by investors, and there is no dilution unless the instrument is a convertible, lenders normally require cash flow, personal guarantees, and/or collateral.

The key to using debt is to make sure that the funds can earn a higher return and can help the company to grow—while having the cash flow to make payments as needed. Many billion-dollar entrepreneurs have used scalable debt to grow at high rates. They made sure that they had the cash flow to repay the increased debt needed to finance the growth in assets.

Some debt instruments that allow scalable debt include the following:

- 💰 Floor planning: Floor planning is used to finance larger pieces of equipment, such as cars and machinery, that are carried as inventory by dealers. The loan is repaid when the inventory is sold.

- 💰 Installment financing: Installment financing is offered to customers by vendors who then sell the note to a financier. It allows customers to buy more expensive durable goods, such as cars, and helps the dealer to sell and to profit from the interest paid.

Other instruments that allow scalable debt include trade credit, line of credit, transaction loans, leases, and factoring (see earlier section).

Conclusion

Knowing the right instruments for each situation can bridge many gaps between financiers and entrepreneurs. It allows financiers to find the right return for the risk they are asked to take. And it allows many entrepreneurs to keep control and balance risk.

Chapter 13

Use VC Intelligently

VC benefits a few at the right time. It is one step to build a billion-dollar venture—for a few. To use VC wisely, you need to be in the right emerging industry and have proven the potential to become a dominating company in the industry or in a sub-segment of the industry. Most importantly, you need to know the right timing, which is after leadership Aha, when dilution is lowest, and before someone else dominates the emerging industry. By doing so, you can control the venture and the industry. By controlling the venture, you create wealth, control the wealth, and reduce dilution.

Many believe that ventures need VC to succeed. Many entrepreneurs consider receiving VC as an endorsement of the venture and, perhaps, a mark of success.

The reality is that VC is only one step in building a high-performance venture. But seeking VC may not be right for you since you may not get VC, or your venture may fail with VC, or you may be fired from the venture by the VCs or by the executives they hire.

I've mentioned the following VC facts which can help you make the right decision about whether to seek VC, delay VC, or avoid VC:

- Ⓢ VCs are very selective
- Ⓢ VCs seek home runs
- Ⓢ VCs seek home runs in emerging industries
- Ⓢ VCs seek to control high-potential ventures
- Ⓢ Few VCs succeed
- Ⓢ Entrepreneurs should avoid or delay VC

VCs Are Very Selective

Reading the business press, it would be reasonable to assume that every entrepreneur can get VC by writing a great business plan. Many intermediaries seek to help entrepreneurs get VC. Incubators and universities organize programs and business plan competitions to connect entrepreneurs with VCs and angels. But is it easy to get VC?

VCs invest in early stage ventures to earn high returns. VC funds get money from pension funds and other large financial institutions that want to earn a high annual return as reasonable compensation for the risks assumed. This means that the VCs seek to invest in a portfolio that earns this high target return for their investors in addition to their own expenses and profit, which is also called "carried interest." But since VC funds invest in high-risk, early stage ventures in emerging industries, many of their investments fail. To earn the required return from a portfolio, VCs target a very high return from each of their investments.

Most Startups Will Not Receive VC

More entrepreneurs ask, "How can I get VC?" rather than "Will I get VC?" The question of how to get VC assumes that entrepreneurs can get VC if only they knew how, or if they knew how to write the perfect business plan and an exquisite elevator pitch.

VCs need to earn a high annual portfolio return of 20 percent and up to offset the high risk in early stage investing. To earn a high portfolio return, VCs seek higher returns from their ventures because of high failure rates. These targets can range from an annual rate of 30 percent for late-stage, lower-risk ventures to more than 80 percent for early stage, high-risk ventures. Very few ventures can offer these high annual returns. As a result, VCs are very selective.

The top-ranked VCs only fund about one or two ventures out of every hundred business plans they see. They reject the rest mainly because they do not see a high reward with acceptable risk.

Depending on the database and time period used, about 600,000+/- businesses are started in the US each year. In 2016, about 1,400 seed-stage deals were funded by VCs (PwcMoneyTree.com). If all seed-stage deals are in year one, this means that the probability of an average new business getting VC is approximately 0.002 percent (assuming one deal per venture).

IMPLICATIONS: Unless you have an exciting breakthrough, or your previous venture was a great success, do not expect VC as a start-up. It's rare for a start-up to get VC, and usually the ones who do receive it demonstrate some evidence that they can dominate a high-potential, emerging market.

Most Ventures Will Not Receive VC

Do the odds change with age? More VC funding is invested as the ventures get older, but the proportion of ventures getting VC is still low. In 2016, there were about 4,800 VC deals (PwCMoneyTree.com). Since these are the number of deals and ventures often receive multiple rounds of funding, the number of ventures getting funding is likely to be below 4,800.

To know your odds of getting VC at a later stage, note that the average age of a venture at VC funding is about four years.[34] This suggests that some were younger than four and others were older. Using a range of zero to eight years, the probability that an average venture will get VC funding is about 0.001 (4,800/4,800,000) assuming 600,000 ventures started per year.

VCs Seek Home Runs

Early stage VCs Need Home Runs for High Returns

Early stage VC is high-risk investing. To compensate for the high risk, early stage VCs seek portfolio returns exceeding 20 percent after expenses. But median VC returns have not kept up with this expectation. Median VC returns have been below the target since the 2000 Internet crash (Figure 5).

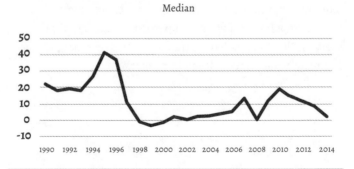

Median

Figure 5. VC returns by year

Source: Cambridge Associates (https://www.quora.com/What-is-the-average-IRR-achieved-by-venture-capital-funds).

VC PORTFOLIO: Many factors affect VC returns, including the following:[35]

💰   Venture mix: This is the proportion of portfolio ventures that are home runs, successes, break-even ventures, partial failures, and total failures.

💰   Investment-per-venture by stage: Ventures are financed in stages as they grow. Ventures that show evidence of potential success receive more investment from VCs in subsequent rounds of financing. These subsequent rounds are usually larger than earlier rounds and have a shorter time to exit and a higher venture valuation, unless it is a down round. Also, the target return for VCs is usually lower in later rounds than in earlier ones.

💰   Years to exit: This can vary depending on the stage of the venture and the frothiness of stock markets. When stock markets are very attractive for IPOs, VCs often exit from their ventures in shorter time periods. Shorter exits can also happen when a large company wants to make a strategic acquisition (see Facebook's acquisition of Instagram about a week after the VC round). Normally, VCs assume that the time to exit is about five to seven years from start-up.

💰   Home runs: The number of home-run ventures has the biggest impact on returns from VC portfolios. But home runs are rare, and the few who invest in them do well.

VCs Seek Home Runs in Emerging Industries

One of the most difficult tasks in business is for entrepreneurs is to build a billion-dollar venture and for VCs is to hit a home run. Since VCs invest in about 100/100,000 ventures and only one of these is likely to be a home run, VCs are careful in their venture selection.

VCs Prefer Disruptive Opportunities

To hit home runs, VCs prefer to invest in high-potential, disruptive opportunities[36] in emerging trends or high-growth industries.[37]

Hamdi Ulukaya built Chobani into a billion-dollar company—without VC. When his father suggested that he start a dairy-products company due to the shortage of "good" dairy products in the US, Ulukaya jumped into the industry, bought plants that were closed, and started his company with debt. He did not use VC. Dairy products are not considered disruptive.

Nondisruptive products in mature industries can be copied by incumbent companies and may not offer entrepreneurs a sufficient advantage to build new giants.

Hamdi Ulukaya seems to be a lucky exception. By not entering the market until Chobani had a significant market share, the incumbent yogurt companies allowed Chobani the space to grow without barriers and belatedly introduced their own brand of Greek yogurt. Also, since yogurt is not a high priority industry for VC funds, Ulukaya grew without VC-funded competitors.

VCs mainly fund high-potential, disruptive opportunities in emerging industries that can offer them high returns. Disruptive ventures such as Amazon.com have used emerging technologies and new business models to get an edge over existing corporations. Amazon.com disrupted many markets and made it difficult for brick-and-mortar stores such as Borders and Sears to copy its strategy of selling online. To combat such disruptive ventures, *larger companies often acquire successful ventures in emerging industries*, giving VCs an attractive exit.

eBay's acquisition of PayPal is an example of an established company buying a growing venture in a new industry.

But there are few attractive, high-potential, disruptive opportunities. Therefore, VCs invest in very few ventures. If your opportunity is not likely to dominate an emerging industry, the probability of getting VC is small.

VCs Prefer Emerging Industries

VCs do well when they invest in the emerging stages of high-growth ventures that create large amounts of wealth. It is easier for ventures to grow rapidly and create large amounts of wealth when they dominate high-potential, high-growth, emerging industries. Emerging industries are often caused by revolutionary trends.

Pierre Omidyar founded eBay in 1995 at the dawn of the Internet age. In 1996, the company held 250,000 auctions. In November 1996, Omidyar found a customer who sold travel products and the number of auctions grew to two million in January 1997. Later that year, after growth was evident and when the industry was emerging, he got his first VC investment of $6.7 million. The company went public in September 2008 and was instantly worth billions. That's what happens in the emerging stages of high-potential multi-billion-dollar industries. The VC investment was worth $2.4 billion, making it one of the best VC investments of all time on an annualized return basis—until Instagram.

Figure 5 shows VC industry returns for 1990–2014, which roughly coincides with Internet 1.0, the emergence of the Internet, Internet 2.0, and the growth of social networking. The returns soared when the industry started to build giant companies such as Google and eBay, and then cooled down until the networking sites took off.

Internet 2.0 did not make as much of a dent as Internet 1.0, perhaps because there were not that many home runs in that period. The amount of VC funding[38] and its returns soar when high-potential industries are emerging.[39] At other times, VC funding and returns fall.

The reason for this fluctuation in VC returns is that emerging high-potential industries create new business giants and billion-dollar fortunes, allowing VCs to earn high returns. But without new, emerging industries, it is difficult to find high-potential ventures.

Bob Kierlin, a billion-dollar entrepreneur, is the founder of Fastenal, the largest US seller of nuts and bolts.[40] At the age of eleven, Kierlin designed a vending machine to sell nuts and bolts. He then finished his education, did a stint in the Peace Corps, and started working for IBM. At this time, he returned to his dream to sell nuts and bolts via a vending machine and started Fastenal. In the first two weeks, he realized that the idea was not feasible at that time. He changed the business strategy to a retail store selling nuts and bolts. He financed the company with $31,000 from his own savings and with money from his friends. He did not seek VC, and VCs were unlikely to invest in a business that sold nuts and bolts because it was not in an emerging industry and had no obvious advantage such as a new technology or a disruptive business model. Kierlin dominated the fragmented industry because he was a stronger competitor. He grew with internal financing.

Jill Blashack Strahan dropped out of college because she wanted to "connect the dots" of what she was learning.[41] When her son was born, Blashack Strahan closed her gift-basket business which required long hours but resulted in earnings of less than $6,000 per year. Then she got the inspiration to sell exceptional convenience foods through home parties. Blashack Strahan bootstrapped the business with a total of $36,000 which she obtained from her personal savings, a partner, and a $20,000 Small Business Administration loan. By 2008, Tastefully Simple's sales were in excess of $140 million, the company was debt free, and Blashack Strahan continued to hold 70 percent of the company. Blashack Strahan did not seek nor was she offered VC because the gift industry was mature, and her business idea was not disruptive.

IMPLICATIONS: VCs prefer opportunities in the growth stages of emerging, high-potential industries because that's where the high-potential opportunities exist. Companies such as Fastenal and Tastefully Simple grew because they were led by exceptional entrepreneurs—not because of the nature of the opportunities. While a few VCs may earn high returns from occasional hits, the VC industry suffers when high-potential industries are not emerging and creating attractive opportunities.

VCs Seek Ventures that Can Dominate the Emerging, High-Potential Industries

VCs seek ventures that can potentially dominate emerging, multi-billion-dollar markets. They reject about 99 percent of plans they see. Nearly every venture seeking VC, including Google, has been turned down by VCs because the potential is not always obvious before Aha.

In fact, Google was rejected by twelve VCs and by a company that could have bought it for a million dollars. A VC from Bessemer

Venture Partners was visiting a friend who had rented her garage to Brin and Page. She volunteered to introduce the VC to these two entrepreneurs. He turned down the offer.[42] In fact, his actual words were, *"How can I get out of this house without going anywhere near your garage?"*

IMPLICATIONS: VCs need to see high returns. To see high returns, VCs seek to finance ventures that show evidence that they can dominate emerging, high-potential industries.

VCs Prefer Ventures with Attractive Exit Options

To earn the high portfolio returns and the high targeted venture returns, VCs like fast, attractive exits—with high annual returns. Few ventures get fast, attractive exits.

In early April 2012, Instagram raised $50 million at a valuation of $500 million. A few days later, on April 12, Facebook bought Instagram for about a billion dollars.[43] Instagram had 30 million users who paid nothing for the service.[44] Another source notes that Instagram had "lots of buzz and no business model."[45] Instagram is very unusual for giving its investors such a fast exit, but it shows that VCs like fast, attractive exits.

VCs have the exit in mind when they invest. Ventures that are highly successful to VCs offer high-value exits via initial public offerings (IPOs) or strategic sales to large corporations. These exits are attractive due to their higher valuations.

IPOs like eBay and strategic sales like Instagram are the leading examples of highly profitable exits. Ventures without the potential of attractive IPOs or strategic sales are unlikely to get VC funding because they are not seen as offering high returns and are therefore less desirable.

Few ventures are likely to have attractive IPOs, and there are more IPOs when markets are in a state of "irrational exuberance"

as in the late 1990s. From 1980 to 2000, an average of 311
companies went public each year. Since then, the number has
fallen to 105 in 2016 and 160 in 2017.[46] This compares with about
600,000 new startups each year and 27 million businesses in the
US. Regarding strategic sales, few ventures have the strategic
value that entices corporations to pay a high price.

Mark Cuban built Broadcast.com and sold it to Yahoo for $5.7
billion in Yahoo stock. When it was sold, the company was said to
have sales close to $100 million.[47] This is the stuff that dreams are
made of and an example of a high-value exit to a strategic buyer.
But they don't happen frequently.

In contrast, the billion-dollar entrepreneurs interviewed for
this book had high aspirations, such as Dick Schulze's goal of a
billion dollars in sales for Best Buy. But these entrepreneurs did
not expect an IPO at the start. Most were not even thinking of an
"exit." As they grew, some sold at high valuations. Others stayed
to lead giant companies. Some went public. Most stayed private.

For a high-value IPO, it helps if you are a hot venture in a
potentially hot emerging industry. For a high-value strategic
sale, check to see who can benefit the most from your strategic
advantage, or who purchased your direct competitors and
whether your valuation is likely to be comparable.

If your venture is not expected to have an attractive exit option,
you are unlikely to get VC. Don't seek VC if your goal is to stay
private, since staying private does not help VCs exit with a high
annual return.

Conclusion

99.9 percent don't get VC and 0.8 percent fail with it. The
remaining 0.02 percent should delay VC to stay in control of their
venture and the wealth created. Even with VC, you may fail. And

even if you succeed with VC, you may lose control of your venture and the wealth it could create.

VCs often get their money out first—by investing in preferred stock and getting warrants and convertibility to buy common stock. Entrepreneurs get to share in the remainder with the VCs and the management team that the VCs often hire.

VCs Seek to Control High-Potential Ventures

VCs have fiduciary obligations to their funders. This means that they have to use their expertise to try and make the venture successful and guide the venture. To make sure that the entrepreneur listens to their guidance or replaces the entrepreneur with a proven executive, VCs like to control the direction of the venture and its leadership.

VC Is Expensive and Controlling Before Aha

Entrepreneurs need to select the right time to seek VC. This timing has profound implications for the venture and for the entrepreneur. It is difficult for investors to identify future home runs before the venture can offer evidence. Seek VC too early before your high potential is evident, and you may waste a lot of time seeking VC. Seek it too late, and others may pass you by.

If you need VC, pick 'Goldilocks' time—not too hot nor too cold—when your potential is evident but before the peloton has passed you by.

Should you:

- 💰 Seek VC early and lose time?

💰   Seek VC as soon as your opportunity's potential is evident and lose control?

💰   Seek VC after your opportunity's potential and your leadership skills are evident and stay in charge?

💰   Grow without VC and avoid dilution?

While VCs fund many deals, entrepreneurs may not have more than one great idea, and they may be better off acquiring skills to delay VC and stay in control of the venture.

In general, seek VC after Aha—if you need it. Not all billion-dollar entrepreneurs needed VC or got it. In fact, 76 percent did not get VC. And only about 25 percent of the billion-dollar entrepreneurs who got VC got it early. Billion-dollar entrepreneurs mainly grew by avoiding VC or delaying it. If you seek VC before leadership Aha, others are likely to control your venture. Seek VC as a fuel for growth after you have proven your potential, and you may dominate your market and as well as control your venture and the fortune it creates.

This was the difference between Jobs I and Jobs II. After starting Apple with Steve Wozniak, Jobs I got VC early and lost control. He was booted out of Apple. But when Apple was failing, Jobs, who had proven his skills at Pixar, was invited back to turn Apple around. He did—all the way to the top of the world. Jobs II was heralded as one of the greatest entrepreneurs in history when he built Apple into a giant with the iPod, the iPhone, and the iPad. But history does not give many people a second bite of the same Apple.

VCs Seek Control

Although early-stage VCs mostly invest after proof of the opportunity's potential, the risks are still high since it is not clear whether the venture can dominate the emerging industry. Due to the high risks and their negotiating clout, VCs usually seek to control the venture and its strategic decisions.

Segway is a good example of the risk. VCs invested about $100 million in the venture.[48] Segway did not succeed and was sold to a British entrepreneur.[49] The inventor had predicted that the Segway *"will be to the car what the car was to the horse and buggy."*[50] Obviously, it wasn't. VCs do gamble and lose.

Since no one is perfect, and this includes the top VCs, ceding strategic control to investors who impose their vision may not be better than implementing your own. Also, when entrepreneurs lose control to the VCs, they may not have any influence on the venture.

Zuckerberg was finance smart. Since he had already proven Facebook's growth and potential and developed a successful business model VC, he obtained VC after proving his leadership skills and was able to control the VCs.

Should you cede control to VCs? For entrepreneurs, getting VC early means losing control of the venture and being diluted by VCs and by the professional managers recruited by the VCs. If the venture is that rarest of ventures, a home run, entrepreneurs usually do well along with the VCs and professional managers, if any. But in ventures that do not become home runs, entrepreneurs may not do well since VCs have preference.

If VC is needed, get it after finding the right strategy and developing a compelling track record, i.e. after leadership Aha. Then add VC as fuel to grow with the proven strategy—unless you can grow without VC.

VCs Prefer Professional Managers who Replace Entrepreneurs

To cut their risk, VCs seek the right leadership. To do so, they like to recruit corporate leaders to manage the venture or fund previously successful entrepreneurs. The percent of entrepreneurs being replaced by professional managers is estimated to be as low as 20 percent[51] while some have pegged this number at around 50 percent. Among companies started by billion-dollar entrepreneurs, only 6 percent of the founders are replaced by a non-founder CEO.

Steve Jobs was fired from Apple in favor of professional CEOs who put Apple on the path to destruction. Apple improved and succeeded after Jobs returned.

Bill Gates, however, delayed VC until after it was evident that Microsoft would be a giant company. He had no trouble attracting VC and staying in control.

VC-backed ventures with professional CEOs rarely made their entrepreneurial founders into billion-dollar entrepreneurs. The reasons may include the venture's failure, dilution, or an early exit to satisfy VC needs.

VCs also recruit leaders by stages and seek CEOs who fit the stage of the venture. An excellent paper by Pascal Levensohn highlights this transition.[52] At the start-up stage, VCs seek leaders who can develop the product, bring it to market, and recruit the right team. At the emerging stage, VCs seek leaders who can guide and control the company after it takes off. At the growth stage, they seek leaders who can build the business into a major corporation and take it public or position it for a high-value sale to a strategic buyer.

VCs hope that professional managers or previously successful entrepreneurs can recreate their magic. The lesson for you as an entrepreneur is to continuously learn what you need to grow to the next stage—if you want to stay in control of your venture.

> **NOTE:** If the venture takes off immediately, everyone may win. However, ventures do not take off as soon as VCs invest because the emerging industry may not take off immediately. There can be a lag between the start of an industry and its take off, and this lag can be more than three years from introduction of a revolutionary product till take off.[53] Ventures that find the key to jumpstarting the emerging industry will be the first ones taking off and spurring the growth of the industry. Ventures that don't keep up with the leaders as they take off may be liquidated or sold. Can you do better by staying in control until the growth strategy is proven and there is proof of take off?

IMPLICATIONS: High-performance entrepreneurs usually prefer to keep control of their venture. Seventy-five percent of billion-dollar entrepreneurs who got VC delayed getting it until after Aha and kept control. The key question for you if you are considering VC is whether your venture and you would fare better with professional management controlled by VCs. If the early results are not satisfactory, VCs and the managers may lose interest and leave, which may cause the venture to wither. Can you bring momentum back to your venture if that happens?

VCs Seek Preference over Entrepreneurs

Even when VCs earn attractive returns, which happens in about 19 percent of funded ventures, it may be at the expense of the entrepreneurs.

Rollerblade is a good example of investors doing well while the entrepreneurs did not.[54] Rollerblade was started by Scott Olson, the inventor of inline skates. When he needed financing, he got it from an investor. The history of the company gets complicated with claims, counter claims, and lawsuits. Finally, the investor sold his share of the company for about $150 million. Olson was not as fortunate when it came to his final settlement.[55]

VCs usually use a financial instrument called the convertible preferred share under which their investment, dividend, and often gain is "preferred" over other investors and the entrepreneurs. Sometimes, the VCs get a multiple of their investment before anyone else gets a dime, and they may dip into whatever is remaining for an additional share of profits. In a failure, they get their share of the cash first. Entrepreneurs usually come last. In about 80 percent to 99 percent of VC-funded ventures, the entrepreneurs may get only their salaries, which are usually lower than corporate salaries.

A further complication is that capital-intensive growth usually needs ongoing funding. Entrepreneurs often do not have the resources to invest in these additional rounds, but VCs do. This could result in further dilution to entrepreneurs. Ventures that do not meet expectations often do not have too many financing options and have to go through what used to be called the "cram-down" round[v] where entrepreneurs often lose more. The net result is that entrepreneurs are likely to see a strong payday only in home runs like eBay and Google. These are rare; however, they are the ones that are continually publicized.

IMPLICATIONS: Since home runs are estimated to compose about one percent of VC-funded ventures, entrepreneurs may not gain much from their venture in about 99 percent of VC-funded

---

v   Cram down means that the value of the venture has fallen from previous rounds of financing and the VCs invest more money for a much lower valuation than in the previous round. It is highly dilutive to existing shareholders. The term is not popular after some VCs lost a lawsuit filed by entrepreneurs who claimed they were unfairly crammed down

deals. These entrepreneurs may do better by learning to grow without, or with delayed, VC.

VCs Cull the Herd

VCs want proof of potential and target their returns based on evidence of this proof. They seek higher annual returns in earlier stages (as noted before) when risk is higher and accept lower returns in later stages as risk is reduced. The proportion of VC funding increases by stage as noted for 2016:[56]

- 💰 Seed Stage: Approximately two to four percent of VC funds are invested at this stage.

- 💰 Early-Stage: About 20 percent.

- 💰 Expansion Stage: About 30 percent.

- 💰 Later Stage: About 40 percent (the rest of VC investments are classified as other).

VCs add coal to a burning fire. They mainly invest after you get to Aha where the venture's potential is evident. Given that about 96 percent to 98 percent of VC investments are post-seed stage, it is evident that their primary strategy is to invest in companies that have already developed some proof of momentum to dominate a high-growth, high-potential emerging industry. For entrepreneurs who seek VC, this practice implies that they have to reach Aha without VC and seek VC after Aha if they cannot grow without VC.

Few VCs Succeed

Policy makers and entrepreneurs seem to be constantly lamenting the "shortage" of early-stage VC funding to build businesses. They give the impression that all you need to develop successful businesses is more capital. If there were really a shortage of VC, then all VCs should earn high returns because all VCs should be able to fund home runs.

But is this true? Are all VCs successful all the time and everywhere? Or are only a handful successful, at certain times, and in certain places? Is there a hierarchy of VCs? If there is a hierarchy, who are the most successful VCs, and how should you select one of them if VC is right for you? Will they fund you?

Home Runs Are Rare

It is easy to believe from the press that VCs invest in nothing but home runs like eBay or Instagram.

eBay is one of the most successful home runs of all time when measured on an annual IRR basis. About $7 million invested in eBay was worth $2.4 billion in eighteen months, an annual return of about 5,000 percent.[57] As noted earlier, Instagram may have a better annual return, with a 100 percent return in one week. The average internal rate of return (IRR) from seven other home runs in the 1980s was 781 percent.[58]

But home runs are rare, even in Silicon Valley which has one of the highest concentrations of home runs in the history of venture capital.

The industry estimates that about one percent of VC-funded ventures become home runs. An additional 19 percent are said to be successes. About 20 percent to 40 percent of VC-funded ventures are said to be total losses, with the remainder being partial losses or barely breaking even.

Marc Andreessen, cofounder of Netscape and VC-firm Andreessen Horowitz, has noted that "*97 percent of venture capital returns come from fifteen investments.*"[59] The statement refers to his belief that only about fifteen ventures each year are home runs and create most of the VC profits for the year. If this number is correct, the probability of your venture becoming a home run is about 0.000025 (15/600,000). This means that about 99.997 percent of entrepreneurs will not become home runs and may be better off without VC.

Venture capitalist Howard Anderson notes that the "common wisdom" in the VC industry is that of every hundred ventures financed, twenty are total write-offs, twenty are losers, forty are in the middle, and twenty are winners.[60]

PwCMoneytree.com notes that there were 54,747 VC deals between 1995 and 2008. Some of these investments were likely to be follow-on rounds of financing, so the number of ventures may be lower. In the same period, there were about 1,450–1,500 VC-backed IPOs for an annual average of about 103–106 (the number is an approximate range based on estimated numbers from a graph).[61] This suggests that under 3 percent of VC-backed ventures went public.

IMPLICATIONS: The key point to note is that the VC model needs home runs to pay for many losses or partial successes. But if VCs had more than one percent to two percent of home runs in a portfolio, the VC returns would have exceeded the actual historical numbers. This means that the VC model works for a few VCs and entrepreneurs, and only under certain conditions. The question for you, the entrepreneur, is whether your venture will be one of the fifteen to sixty VC home runs per year. And if you do have a home run, how much of the wealth created will you keep?

Emerging Industries Create Home Runs

Home runs are rare because they are not created in a vacuum. VC home runs are mainly created in high-growth, high-potential, emerging industries.

When VCs have tried to create new industries without a breakthrough technology, they have mostly failed. After the dotcom bust of 2000, some VC funds such as Kleiner Perkins invested to *create* a "green" industry. They did not succeed at the time. One investor noted that "they have stopped drinking the Kool-Aid and are committing to coming back and focusing on making money again."[62]

VCs do best in emerging, high-potential industries because high-growth, high-value ventures are more likely to be developed in such industries. By their definition, emerging industries also do not have strong, established direct competitors.

VC-favored industries have changed over time as emerging industries mature and newer ones emerge. If VCs invest in mature industries such as the medical-device industry they fund ventures that seek to dominate new niche markets. They usually sell the successful ventures to larger, more established medical-device corporations rather than seeking an IPO. These medical ventures can be considered to be external R&D for the companies in the mature industries.

Table 2. Home Runs by Timing and Emerging Industry

Time	Industry	Home Runs (year founded)
'60s	Semiconductors	Intel (1968), AMD (1969)
'70s	PCs	Apple (1976), Microsoft (1975)
'70s–'80s	Biotech	Genentech (1976), Amgen (1980)
'80s–'90s	Telecom/ Optics	Cisco (1984), Ciena (1992)
'90s	Internet	eBay (1994), Google (1998)
'00s	Internet 2.0	Facebook (2004), Twitter (2006)

In the past fifty years, many new industries have created home runs. These industries and the new markets they created, such as semiconductors in the 1960s and 1970s, personal computers and software in the 1970s, biotechnology in the 1970s and early 1980s, telecom in the 1980s and 1990s, Internet 1.0 in the 1990s, and Internet 2.0 in the 2000s, created home runs such as Intel, AMD, Apple, Google, and Facebook. Table 2 shows the timing of emerging industries and some of the home runs created in those industries.

The impact of these home runs can be seen in the returns from VC funds with various vintages:

- **⑤** Returns ranged from 42.9 percent for funds started in the 1990–96 era to -9.77 percent for funds started between 1998–2008.63

- **⑤** Returns were very high for funds that were started in 1994 (49.6 percent per year) and 1997 (67.5 percent) due to their investments in the Internet.64

IMPLICATIONS: To get high returns, VCs need home runs. To get home runs, VCs need emerging industries.

Few VCs Succeed Because Home Runs Are Rare

Most VCs have mediocre returns. An analysis of VC fund returns shows that four percent of 1,200 VC firms accounted for 66 percent of market value from IPOs between 1997 and 2001.[65] As noted earlier, Andy Rachleff, formerly of Benchmark Partners, notes that twenty VC firms (about 3 percent) earn about 95 percent of the VC industry's returns.[66]

Annual returns over twenty years for 904 VC funds show that only the top quartile had an annual return above 20 percent.[67] This is because the top quartile returns are benefitting from the returns from the top twenty funds. VC funds not in the top half had very low returns on investment.[68]

Early stage VCs do well when they are an early round investor in home runs. Given that there are hundreds of VC funds in the US and an estimated fifteen to sixty home-run ventures in an average year, most VCs are unlikely to invest in even a single home run. The ones who invest in one or more home runs will have attractive returns. The others will not be as fortunate. Note that most home runs have multiple VC investors.

IMPLICATIONS: A few VCs account for most of the VC industry's profits. The rest have mediocre results. Entrepreneurs who get funding from the top four percent of VC funds have better odds than those who obtain money from others. If you are planning on getting VC and ceding control to VCs in hopes of a home run, get VC from a fund in the top fifty. These top VCs seem to be better at growing winners, but even they do it rarely—so beware. They have offices in Silicon Valley because that's where the home runs are located. If you cannot get money from them, grow without VC or delay VC and stay in control.

Silicon Valley Has Many Home Runs

Silicon Valley is the vanguard of VC and practically the only area where VC home runs are being developed on a consistent basis. Silicon Valley accounts for the following:[69]

- 💰 52 percent of the fifty top VC-backed exits in 2012 and 48 percent in 2011.

- 💰 Exit valuation that was 29.1 times the average funding raised for Silicon Valley compared with 12.9 for Southern California, 11.0 for Massachusetts, 9.6 for New York, and 4.2 for Illinois.

💰 $130 billion of exit valuation, which was 86 percent of national aggregate exit valuation, compared with about three billion dollars for second place Southern California.

As noted earlier, exits are very important for high returns. IPOs and strategic sales to large corporations are the primary high-value exits for the VC industry. Of the two, exit valuations are usually higher in IPOs than in strategic sales.[70] Between June 1996 and December 2006, there were a total of 2,123 IPOs. Of these, 585 (28 percent) were in California, and five states (CA, NY, TX, MA, FL) accounted for 1,093 IPOs (51 percent).

> **NOTE:** Many governments, including the US government, have tried to jump-start ventures in various areas by encouraging early stage VC funds. Nearly all these programs have had sub-par results. Participating SBICs were a type of early stage VC fund sponsored by the Small Business Administration (SBA) to offer government financing to early stage ventures. According to the SBA, four Participating Small-Business Investment Companies (SBIC) out of 184, i.e. about 2 percent of the total, accounted for 50 percent of the net profits of the entire group and eight (4 percent) accounted for 75 percent.[71] The Participating SBIC program was terminated due to losses.

Silicon Valley's dominance has been growing for the last fifty years—from semiconductors to Internet 2.0. Silicon Valley also has more IPOs in key industries.[72]

IMPLICATION: This geographic concentration of high-value exits suggests that VC funders who invest in Silicon Valley are more likely to fare better than VCs in other areas.

Avoid or Delay VC

A common belief over the last four decades has been that VC is needed to build giant companies.

Since the 1970s, when the Silicon Valley VC industry developed its present form, its capital-intensive method has been assumed to be the only way to build giant companies. The relentless drumbeat and intense publicity around VCs and their home runs have led to the following:

- 💰 Many entrepreneurs think that VC is key to building a big business.

- 💰 Governments promote the formation of VC funds with the hope of growing their own "industries of the future."

- 💰 Universities and area leaders organize VC forums and design technology-transfer programs with the hope of developing successful ventures, generating wealth, and creating jobs.

- 💰 Corporations open labs in Silicon Valley hoping to catch the magic of revolutionary innovation.

But is using VC a smart strategy for entrepreneurs, governments, or universities? Is a capital-intensive innovation strategy the right one for corporations, especially in emerging industries?

It Is Possible to Build a Billion-Dollar Company Without VC

Entrepreneurs have built giant companies without VC. You may not have heard about many of them because they often do not benefit, financially or otherwise, from announcing their success, especially if they plan to stay a private company. They can fly under the radar and keep their size, strength, and wealth a secret until they are ready to announce their accomplishments. They also do not have to share their business plans with—or disclose their business secrets to—the world. VCs, on the other hand, seek publicity for themselves and their portfolio companies because it promotes the venture's exit value in an initial public offering or strategic sale. And promoting their home runs helps VCs raise their next funds more easily.

Kevin Plank started Under Armour when he completed his undergraduate studies at the University of Maryland in 1996. As a football player, he noted that the fabric in his compression shorts kept him dry while his T-shirts got soaked. When he finished his undergraduate studies, he founded Under Armour in his grandmother's basement and started selling to football teams. He did not take a salary from his firm for nine years.[73] From this start, and without VC, Plank built Under Armour to annual sales of more than $2.3 billion and a market capitalization of more than $11 billion (as of February 5, 2014).[74]

The common factor among billion-dollar entrepreneurs such as Kevin Plank, Amancio Ortega of Zara, Michael Dell of Dell, Dick Schulze of Best Buy, Steve Ells of Chipotle, and Michael Bloomberg of Bloomberg was something very simple and very difficult to implement for most entrepreneurs who do not take the time and effort to learn how to do it. They used finance as a weapon to build their business, beat their competitors, and control their venture and the wealth created. They were able to do this by avoiding or delaying VC.

Billion-Dollar Entrepreneurs Avoid, or Delay, VC

Billion-dollar entrepreneurs are rare. To understand how small the number is of entrepreneurs who built a company to more than a billion dollars in sales and valuation, consider this: only about 0.01 percent of US companies (2,600 out of about 27 million businesses in the US) have sales in excess of one billion dollars.[vi] Even fewer businesses also had valuation of more than a billion dollars. And the number where the entrepreneur was involved from start-up to billion-dollar status is extremely small. Best estimates are that there are about one hundred to two hundred billion-dollar entrepreneurs in the US. We found eighty-five who got VC early, VC late, or avoided VC (Table 3).

VC EARLY ENTREPRENEURS get VC early and lose control to a CEO picked by the VCs. Steve Jobs got VC early. He cofounded Apple when he was twenty-one. Apple got early angel capital, and then VC as the venture started to take off in the PC revolution. But Jobs was fired from his company when the Macintosh failed to live up to expectations. About six percent of America's billion-dollar entrepreneurs belong in this group, including Pierre Omidyar of eBay.

Table 3. VC Early, VC Late and VC Avoiders

	VC Early	**VC Late**	**VC Avoider**
Leadership	Hired CEO	Founding Entrepreneur	Founding Entrepreneur
Percent of 85 BDEs in sample	6 percent	18 percent	76 percent
Examples	Jobs, Omidyar	Gates, Zuckerberg	Dell, Schulze

VC LATE ENTREPRENEURS get VC after the venture has momentum and its potential is evident, and the entrepreneurs have the credibility to stay on as CEO. At this point, the venture often has options due to interest from many VCs. Since VC Late entrepreneurs stay on as CEO, they are not diluted by the incoming CEO. About 18 percent of America's billion-

---

vi   Dun & Bradstreet Million Dollar database

dollar entrepreneurs delayed VC, including Mark Zuckerberg of Facebook.

Bill Gates got VC late. He cofounded Microsoft in 1976 with Paul Allen. When IBM decided to get into PCs, Gates bought an operating system and licensed it to IBM. He then licensed the operating system to IBM-clone manufacturers. He got VC after Microsoft was in a growth mode and did not lose control of the company.

VC AVOIDERS grow without VC. These entrepreneurs learn how to grow without VC and keep control of their business and of the fortune they create. An astounding 76 percent of America's billion-dollar entrepreneurs were VC Avoiders, including Michael Bloomberg of Bloomberg and Dick Schulze of Best Buy.

Michael Dell was a VC Avoider. He started Dell in his dorm room as a freshman at the University of Texas at Austin. He later went into the business full time in 1984 at the age of nineteen. He sold PCs and accessories from his condo and built the business on his own and with family money. He never got VC and has controlled his company ever since.

CONCLUSION: Contrary to myth, VC does not guarantee success. All it means is that by getting VC early, you may have ceded control of your business to investors whose interests may not mesh with yours. Finance-smart skills and strategies can help you grow without VC or with delayed VC, thereby enabling you to control the business and the wealth you create.

Delay VC in Silicon Valley

There are two Americas (Table 4). In Silicon Valley, about 90 percent of the billion-dollar entrepreneurs used VC. Outside Silicon Valley, about 90 percent of the billion-dollar entrepreneurs grew without VC. This means that entrepreneurs can, and have, built giant businesses without VC, but mainly outside Silicon Valley.

Table 4. Percentage of U.S. Billion Dollar Companies Receiving VC by Region

	VC Early	**VC Late**	**No VC**
Silicon Valley	25 percent	63 percent	12 percent
Outside Silicon Valley	1 percent	8 percent	91 percent
US	6 percent	18 percent	76 percent

This was confirmed in Minnesota.[75] Minnesota has developed one of the highest number per capita of Fortune 500 companies, and one of the highest number per capita of billion-dollar entrepreneurs in the country. In Minnesota, none of the billion-dollar entrepreneurs got VC at the start. Twenty percent attained it after going public, which is quite unique. One company got into financial trouble after going public and got funding from a late-stage VC. 80 percent of the Minnesota billion-dollar entrepreneurs never got VC.

ő   Dick Schulze started Best Buy, the world's largest consumer electronics retailer, that has with more than $40 billion in revenues, with only $9,000 in equity and no VC.[76]

ő   Richard Burke built UnitedHealth Group into the world's largest private healthcare-management company to more than $190 billion in annual sales.[77] He did it without VC and borrowed $40,000 to start the business.

IMPLICATIONS: VCs have built many billion-dollar companies in Silicon Valley. But outside Silicon Valley, giant companies were mainly built without VC.

Avoid VC outside Silicon Valley

Obviously, most entrepreneurs do not become billion-dollar entrepreneurs. Some become hundred-million-dollar entrepreneurs.

In Minnesota (Figure 6), VC has not been very prevalent among even hundred-million-dollar entrepreneurs. Among Minnesota's hundred-million-dollar entrepreneurs, 88 percent never used VC in their first venture. Of the three who did use VC, two got it after Aha and kept control of their venture. One got VC too early and lost control. Today, he wants nothing to do with venture capital.

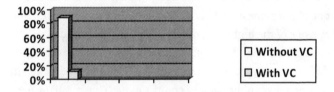

Figure 6. Use of VC by Hundred-Million-Dollar Entrepreneurs

Ed Flaherty of Rapid Oil Change built his company without VC.[78] As he was building his software company in Minneapolis, he found that service stations expected him to leave his car there all day to get his oil changed. He imitated an innovative model from California where they did it faster. He leased a gas station and started the first Rapid Oil Change. The chain grew and Flaherty soon sold to one of the major oil companies.

Should you seek VC if you have a modest goal? You will have four strikes against you:

💰 The top VC funds are not interested in modest visions. They want potential blockbusters to make up for the large proportion of failures in their portfolio and to get good portfolio returns.[vii]

  💰 The lower tier of VC funds that are smaller may finance modest visions. But usually, they do not have a track record of building home runs. This means that you may have to give up control of your dream to VCs who don't have a proven track record of success.

  💰 VCs get their money out first, so they may do well even when others involved in the business do not.

  💰 VCs like to hire a professional CEO who may fire you from your venture and dilute your financial stake. You may end up with little to show for your venture.

IMPLICATIONS: VCs have strict criteria. *If your goal is modest, you may not get VC from the top VC funds and you may not want VC from the others.* Seeking to grow without VC may be a better option. Entrepreneurs outside Silicon Valley may have no choice because they may not be able to get VC.

Control to Keep the Wealth You Create

VCs like to control the venture, although they have not demanded this in some recent home runs such as Facebook because the potential was evident and the entrepreneurs had many options for VC in Silicon Valley. If you want to control your venture, you need to avoid VC or delay it.

---

vii   A "typical" VC portfolio has about 1 percent home runs and 19 percent successes; the remaining 80 percent fail to meet the minimum thresholds for VC success, which is to get a portfolio return of 20 percent per year. In ventures that do not meet the minimum thresholds, VCs are likely to get most of the gain, if any. There may not be much left over for the hired managers and entrepreneurs. For more on this, see "Designing successful venture capital funds for area development: Bridging the hierarchy and equity gaps" by the author, *Applied Research in Economic Development*, 2006 Volume 3, No. 2.

Losing control can affect the proportion of wealth kept by the entrepreneur (Table 5). VC Early means that the entrepreneur will be diluted by the VCs and by the hired executives. VC Late means that the entrepreneurs are diluted only by the VCs. No VC means that there will be no dilution from VCs or executives, but only from friends, family, angels, and alliances.

Table 5. Net Worth/ Wealth Created for Billion-Dollar Entrepreneurs[viii]

	VC Early	**VC Late**	**No VC**
Wealth Retained/ Wealth Created	7 percent	17 percent	56 percent

The data (see Table 8 in the Appendix) shows that *entrepreneurs kept more of the wealth created by keeping control of the venture—when they avoid or delay VC*. VC Traditionalists got VC early and kept only seven percent of the wealth created. VC Delayers kept 17 percent of the wealth created. VC Avoiders kept 56 percent of the wealth created. Note that these numbers are the share of wealth created. The actual amount of wealth kept by those who got VC may be larger because they were dominating larger markets and built larger companies, although all were billion-dollar entrepreneurs.

DELAY TO CONTROL: The key conclusion here is that if you need VC to compete, delaying helps you stay in control and keep more. If you absolutely need VC because you are in an emerging industry and your direct competitors have VC, or because you do not want to bootstrap, then delay getting VC until take off is evident.

SHARE OF WEALTH: By building momentum before seeking VC, billion-dollar entrepreneurs are better able to demonstrate their venture's potential to dominate an emerging industry. This attracts

---

viii   Wealth kept: Entrepreneur's net worth between 2010 and 2012; Wealth created: Venture's market capitalization; data for 21 entrepreneurs whose personal net worth is available from public sources. Note that sources may be approximating some of the numbers

VCs and gives the entrepreneurs additional negotiating clout, which helps them stay on as CEOs. In non-VC-financed industries, entrepreneurs have avoided VC because they did not need it.

Mark Zuckerberg started Facebook from his dorm room. His first professional financing was $500,000 in May 2004 from a Silicon Valley angel, Peter Thiel, who was excited about Facebook's growth.[79] Zuckerberg got his first institutional VC round in May 2005.[80] By then, Facebook had millions of users and was recruiting hundreds of thousands of new users per month. By waiting to get institutional VC until his venture's potential was evident, Zuckerberg could demand control.[81]

ODDS OF SUCCESS: You may also improve your odds of success by growing without VC or with delayed VC. A venture that may have succeeded with entrepreneurial passion and capital efficiency may fail with capital intensity and VC. There were 2.5 times as many VC Delayers as those who got VC early in Silicon Valley. And there were 8 times as many VC Delayers as those who got VC early outside Silicon Valley (see Table 4). By delaying, the billion-dollar entrepreneurs stayed in control.

VC Advice May Be No Better than Other Advice

VCs often suggest that one advantage to working with them is the advice they offer. Do VCs give good advice? Does their advice benefit the entrepreneur?

When you consider the fact that only about one to two percent of VC-funded ventures become home runs, shouldn't you question why the other 98 percent to 99 percent of VC-funded ventures are not home runs and why VCs fail on 80 percent of their ventures?[ix] Do VCs succeed due to luck or skill? Are the home runs the result

---

ix   Note that the precise number of whether home runs are 1 percent or 2 percent of a "typical" VC portfolio is not as important as the fact that about 98–99 percent are not. If there were more than 2 percent home runs, VC returns would exceed historical averages as they did during the dotcom boom.

of good VC advice, the uniqueness of the opportunity, or some other factor?

While VCs can develop attractive networks due to their potential for creating wealth, claims about the quality of VC advice may be overrated. For example, post-investment involvement of VCs does not significantly affect venture performance, and angels may offer better help.[82] The reason for the possibly higher quality of angel advice could be that many angels have managed and built businesses. They know how to grow a business. VCs often have professional backgrounds and may not have built successful businesses themselves.

Perhaps the real problem with offering advice to new ventures is that there are too many unknowns about the technology, strength of competitors, viability of the advantage, rate of acceptance, and a hundred other variables and decisions. Guess wrong on even one, and you may have a failure on your hands.

Even Marc Andreessen who built Netscape and is one of the successful VCs in Silicon Valley was wrong about Instagram.[83] Although his firm Andreesen Horowitz did well in the company, Andreesen invested in a competitor's succeeding rounds, not in Instagram's.

At the end of the day, everyone seems to be guessing about which ventures to fund. The only difference is that the Silicon Valley VCs are guessing in a very fertile field.

IMPLICATIONS: If VC advice were all that potent, shouldn't they succeed in developing more home runs than just in one percent of their investments, shouldn't they make money in both good times and bad, and shouldn't they be successful everywhere? Do you want to risk your venture on someone else's advice or get to Aha without VC and control your direction by developing your skills?

Know the VC Reality

VC is expensive business financing. VCs expect a high return to compensate them for the high risk. And VCs also expect to control the venture. With all of this, is VC worth this cost?

Many entrepreneurs seem to believe that getting VC is a mark of success. But VC comes with strings attached. The question for you is whether you should accept VC if you can get it or whether you should be capital efficient and avoid or delay VC? Know the reality of VC before you get it and lose control.

VCs range from the top fifty Silicon Valley VCs who have invested in home runs to community VCs who invest in low-income areas. The former has experience and money. The latter has little. But the latter may be easier to tap. VC also includes late-stage VCs and SBICs. Except for bank-owned SBICs, most SBICs prefer to invest in late-stage ventures.

Four percent of VCs do well because they fund home runs. They are in Silicon Valley and fund mainly emerging, high-potential industries. Billion-dollar entrepreneurs outside Silicon Valley mainly grew without VC or with delayed VC, and finance-smart expertise helped them do this.

Conclusion

The reality of VC is that very few entrepreneurs benefit from it. In a world obsessed with VC, it is worth noting that more than 9/10 of America's unicorn-entrepreneurs grew without VC outside Silicon Valley and with delayed VC in Silicon Valley. By doing so, they controlled the venture and wealth created.

The early-stage VC way seeks grade A opportunities and recruits grade A executives. But the VC way has worked for only about

0.02 percent of US ventures, mainly in Silicon Valley, and after Aha when potential is evident. There is a *VC-benefit gap* for 99.98 percent of US ventures, a *VC-area gap* outside Silicon Valley, and a *VC-stage gap* from idea till Aha.

About 94 percent of America's eighty-five unicorn-entrepreneurs used finance-smart expertise to bridge the VC-benefit gap, VC-area gap, and VC-stage gap. They used three strategies:

- 💰 VC Traditionalists, who were six percent of BDEs, got VC early after developing a high-potential opportunity. They lost control of their ventures to the VCs, were replaced as CEOs by professional executives, and kept the smallest share of the wealth created among the three categories. Example: Pierre Omidyar of eBay.

- 💰 VC Delayers, who were 18 percent of BDEs, got VC late and took off with finance-smart expertise. They proved their venture's potential and their own leadership skills. They got VC after takeoff, stayed on as CEOs, and kept more of the wealth created than VC Traditionalists. Examples: Bill Gates of Microsoft and Mark Zuckerberg of Facebook.

- 💰 VC Avoiders, who were 76 percent of the group, avoided VC. They used finance-smart expertise to control their venture and kept the largest share of the wealth created. They avoided dilution by VCs and by VC-recruited executives. Examples include Michael Bloomberg of Bloomberg, Richard Schulze of Best Buy, and Richard Burke of UnitedHealthcare.

Chapter 14

Develop the Right Capital Structure

Your capital structure, which includes sources, instruments, and amounts by stage, can influence whether you succeed and control the venture and the wealth created. So, structure with care.

To control the venture, create wealth, and control it, entrepreneurs need to find the right financing at the right stage. To grow with control, evaluate and develop the business holistically by linking the business and finance strategies. This means knowing how your business skills can influence business strategy, how business strategy influences finance strategy, and how finance strategy influences business success and personal wealth. Then, adjust the skills, business strategy, and finance strategy until you find the right direction for you.

Billion-dollar entrepreneurs build a capital-efficient structure using a finance-smart backbone and strategies to grow with control. To do this, they structure to grow with control, which includes the following rules.

Structure for Capital Efficiency

A capital-efficient backbone (Figure 7) should help you develop your growth opportunity, competitive business strategy, controlled finance strategy, and real-time take off to optimize the financial footprint of the entire business.

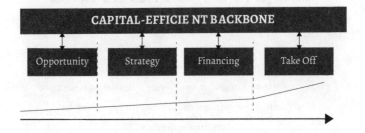

Figure 7. Venture's Financial Backbone

Structure for Uncertainty

The earlier the business stage, the higher the uncertainty. This means that your start-up business plan is just a road map—and hardly ever leads you to success. But it helps to monitor your achievements and adjust. Seek flexibility in your business and financial strategies and adjust with real feedback from your take off strategy. Avoid being locked into a direction until you are certain of its value.

Structure for Control

Once you lose control of your venture, the direction of the business and any wealth created are not under your control either. Seek to delay controlling capital until you can get capital you control. To delay controlling capital, maximize your internal cash flow with finance and business skills until leadership Aha. The common misconception is that high growth not only needs huge amounts of capital, but also causes negative cash flow. However, most billion-dollar entrepreneurs outside Silicon Valley grew with positive cash flow. Capital efficiency can help.

Structure for Self-Funded Working Capital

To self-fund working capital, you will need to consider getting paid by customers before paying your vendors, reducing or eliminating the need for inventory and accounts receivable, and avoiding losses. This can mean redesigning your business from the ground up. In the Internet age, more ventures have been able to develop a self-funding model by selling direct to the consumer and avoiding accounts receivable.

Structure to Avoid Owning Fixed Assets

Fixed assets are usually the easiest to fund from external, non-controlling sources so long as you have the cash flow to make monthly payments to pay the leases or loans. The cost of such fixed-asset financing is usually much lower than the cost of equity.

Structure by Type of Need

Financiers want to know your financial needs for each type of use since each use has its own risk profile and is often financed differently. Your financial needs will depend on your strategy, structure, and business stage. The main uses include the following:

LOSSES: A loss is tough to finance when you are just starting the business. Losses after Aha are easier to fund if you are attractive to VCs. At the start, investors may not be convinced of your opportunity, and lenders are not convinced of your viability. Lenders usually seek additional collateral, such as personal assets, in addition to business collateral. Therefore reduce losses—at least until Aha. After Aha, VC funding may be available to finance losses in ventures that are likely to dominate high-potential, emerging industries, especially in Silicon Valley.

INVENTORY AND RECEIVABLES: Lenders hesitate to finance inventory and accounts receivable in startups due to the risk that they may not be easily converted to cash at full value if the venture goes bankrupt. Therefore, the amount of debt available (loan-to-value) is usually much lower for risky inventory and receivables.

EQUIPMENT: Equipment can be funded with loans, leases, or equity. Loan-to-value ratios are usually lower for special-purpose equipment, requiring the business to use more of its equity or seek vendor financing.

REAL ESTATE: Of the various needs, general-purpose real estate in desirable locations is easiest to finance using loans or leases since the collateral usually has value even if the business fails. Renting till the business has positive cash flow can help reduce equity needs. After you have positive cash flow, you can evaluate the best use for your cash: real estate or growth capital?

Structure by Source

You will benefit from learning about all the financial sources available to your business, their suitability, criteria, and demands, and how you can mix-and-match among your options to find the right ones to grow with control. Financial sources include equity, debt, and government sources, in addition to internal cash flow.

Structure with the Right Instruments

As an entrepreneur, you have many options to choose from including equity, debt, and hybrid instruments. Using the right instrument that matches financiers' criteria with your own needs can help you get the right funding to grow with control.

Structure by Stage

While VCs evaluate the stage of the venture, from R&D to growth and beyond, and lenders examine whether you have positive or negative cash flow, entrepreneurs should be primarily concerned about pre-Aha, pre-leadership Aha, and post-leadership Aha. Before Aha, bootstrapping is the only option since VC is not available. After opportunity Aha and before leadership Aha, you may get VC, but not on your terms. After leadership Aha, you can get VC and stay in control of the venture and the wealth you create.

To stay in control and reduce dilution, the right structure at each stage means selecting the most appropriate combination:

Amounts by use—current assets, fixed assets, and losses

Sources by need—equity, debt, and development finance

Instruments by type—equity, debt, and hybrid

The right structure depends on the following:

- 💰 Proven potential: The greater the proven potential to create wealth, the higher the VC interest

- 💰 Risk: Investors and lenders show more interest in financing when the risk is lower

- 💰 Economy: The cost of money is usually higher when the economy is stronger

- 💰 Location: Some areas might have fewer resources

- 💰 Venture characteristics, including stage, potential, industry growth rate, cash flow, cash needs, and uses of financing

- 💰 Financiers' criteria, including industry, stage, risk, and potential

- 💰 Your goals

A complex financial structure with multiple financial sources and specialized financial instruments may be better for the business since each financing source can be matched with each specific need to obtain the best terms, repayment requirements, and cost. But it may require more time and expertise to raise such financing. A simpler one may be faster to obtain but may not be as good a fit as the business grows.[84]

Structure with the Right Process

Many entrepreneurs assume that the right way to obtain financing for a business is to evaluate a new business idea, develop the strategy and projections, write a business plan, and then seek venture capital.

The finance-smart process to financing would be to:

- 💰 Evaluate a new business idea, develop the strategy and financial projections, write a business plan, and evaluate financial needs

- 💰 Assess the financial sources that are viable, their requirements and costs, and potential loss of control for the entrepreneur

- 💰 If attractive controllable financing is not obtainable, consider the following steps to grow with reduced needs:
  - ‣ Reduce frills and any other easy-to-cut needs
  - ‣ Adjust implementation strategy
  - ‣ Adjust business model and strategy
  - ‣ Adjust the opportunity

- 💰 Develop a new business plan and financial projections

- 💰 Assess financing options again. Repeat.

Conclusion

A sound financing plan that is fitted to your business strategy can help you achieve your goals, create wealth, and control it. Financing is a key resource.

Most entrepreneurs do not have a choice regarding VC. They do not qualify for it and will not get it. The key questions for you are whether you can grow either without VC or with controlled VC.

Here are some reasons to stay in control.

FEW ENTREPRENEURS GAIN FROM VC: Entrepreneurs benefit significantly from VC if their venture becomes a home run. But the probability of getting VC and then becoming a home run is very, very small.

VC MAY BE DETRIMENTAL TO YOUR POTENTIAL WEALTH: Entrepreneurs who want to keep more of the wealth created by their venture should avoid VC, or delay getting it until their business momentum attracts VCs, allowing them to negotiate and stay on as CEOs.

VC HELPS IN SILICON VALLEY: More than 90 percent of Silicon Valley's billion-dollar entrepreneurs were funded by VCs. Outside Silicon Valley, more than 90 percent grew without VC. In Silicon Valley, delay VC. Outside Silicon Valley, learn to grow without VC.

WITHOUT VC, OR WITH DELAYED VC, YOU GET TO CONTROL YOUR EXIT: VCs need to exit from their investments and can usually force companies to go public or to be sold, even if the timing is not favorable to the venture or to the entrepreneur. Without VC, entrepreneurs can decide when and whether to exit.

BUT VC HELPS TO DOMINATE AN EMERGING INDUSTRY: Entrepreneurs are more likely to get VC in emerging industries. Seek VC if you are in an emerging industry, your competitors have VC, and you can get an advantage with it. But even then, delay getting VC until after you have momentum.

STAGE MATTERS. Your cost of money, which is the return sought by investors, depends on the stage of your venture. The target return for investors, which is your cost, can be as high as 80 percent to 100 percent per year in the early high-risk rounds of financing. This target return falls as your venture shows more progress and proof of potential to dominate an attractive growth segment. Make sure that the money you raise will add enough value to your venture to earn more than this high cost.

THE RIGHT VC MATTERS: If you do need VC to stay competitive, get it from the right sources. The top fifty VC funds have the best records and are the most attractive sources to build giant companies. These funds are three times more likely to be accepted by ventures, they get an advantage of 10 percent to 14 percent in entry valuation, and their ventures get better valuations in IPO exits.[x] But even these top VCs have only about fifteen to sixty home runs per year, mainly when high-potential industries are emerging. In the past five years, 98 percent to 100 percent of the top fifty VCs were in Silicon Valley.

It helps to know the financial options available to your business, including the sources and instruments available, their suitability, and how you can mix-and-match your options to find the right ones that help you grow without losing control.

---

[x]   The rationale behind this increased IPO valuation is not clear. One explanation is that investment bankers and the investing public are reassured to know that a top VC is on the board with their funds in the venture. But most VCs like to exit as soon as they can after a venture goes public. Another explanation could be that the top VCs are better negotiators and able to strong-arm investment bankers to offer higher valuations for their ventures. For more, see AVOID VC Intelligently® at www.dileeprao.com

Part III

Post Finance: Controlling to Take Off

The proof of your planning is in your take off. To make sure
the venture can take off with limited cash, you need to use
your skills to launch, monitor, adjust, and succeed. You
need to control your venture in real time to take off with
limited resources.

Unlike capital-intensive VC-funded ventures, most billion-dollar entrepreneurs, especially those outside Silicon Valley, used capital-efficient launch strategies.

How VC-Funded Ventures Take Off

VCs want to fund ventures only where the potential for growth is evident. To seek this potential for growth, VCs are very selective and have very strict criteria.

VCs Seek Hot Ventures in a High-Growth Industry

VCs seek high returns from both their fund and their ventures. To earn high returns, VCs mostly invest huge amounts after the venture shows evidence of potential. VC-backed ventures invest significant amounts to stay at the leading edge of an emerging industry. If the timing, strategy, or execution are not perfect, if some other venture finds the magic formula in the emerging industry, or another giant company imitates the strategy, the venture can fail. This happens about 80 percent of the time. But if the venture continues to live up to its potential and shows the ability to dominate an attractive, high-growth industry, VCs invest more in subsequent rounds in order to develop a home run.

VCs Like to See a Proven Takeoff Strategy

Although both have a tough task, VCs have it easier than entrepreneurs. This is because VCs wait until the entrepreneurs have already done the heavy lifting. The average age of a venture when VCs get involved is about four years.[85] Most VCs invest after the business model is developed and proven, and when the venture is growing with momentum. According to VC statistics, about 96 percent to 98 percent of VC investments are made after the early stage.[86] This means that there are already some signs of potential dominance by the time VCs invest.

It is easier to find VC after the venture shows the potential to dominate an emerging industry. Investors who fund a venture with an attractive opportunity, but before growth momentum, expect management to find the right strategy and execute it. This is why many VCs are fond of saying that "grade B management will kill grade A products, while grade A management can succeed with grade B products." Success is not just about the product or service or app. It is also about the business strategy and execution. But finding the successful strategy is not easy— and can be more difficult when it is done under time pressure and with many chefs.

Groupon's initial business model called The Point promoted "collective activism."[87] When that strategy did not provide the desired results, Groupon shifted to its business model of selling coupons online.

VCs Want Focused Ventures

VCs want their ventures to focus on one market until the venture dominates that market. They want the venture to concentrate its resources to dominate an attractive, fast-growing market, and to diversify after dominating the initial market. As an example, Lyft is still focused on one market, the US. Meanwhile, Uber, run by an entrepreneur with more control, expanded to multiple markets and multiple product lines. Lyft is expected to reach profitability first.

VCs like Direct-To-Customer Models

Until the Internet was introduced, VCs mainly funded companies that sold to other businesses, i.e. they were B2B businesses.

Selling to consumers via indirect channels is both time consuming and expensive, even for VCs. VCs want fast success and a high annual return. Indirect models normally need higher investment on channel development, consumer advertising, and promotion. The indirect method also offers lower gross margins due to the number of intermediaries and results in the venture getting a smaller percent of the sales price. Perhaps most importantly, the venture is not building a direct relationship with the consumer, so it does not often "own" the consumer, which means that the intermediaries can switch to others. Since the Internet allows companies to connect directly with consumers, VCs have embraced Internet-based, direct-to-consumer companies. VC-funded companies that have dominated consumer markets include Amazon, Google, Yahoo, eBay, Uber, and Airbnb. They work directly with consumers.

Hamdi Ulukaya of Chobani is one of the few billion-dollar entrepreneurs who used indirect channels. He offset this disadvantage by focusing on a product, Greek yogurt, that had been overlooked by giants in the food industry, developing great packaging, and initially focusing on retailers who were selling to high-income consumers.

VCs Want Ventures that Can Dominate Their Strategic Group

VCs expect their ventures to lead the industry because industry dominators usually end up winning and achieving the highest valuations. This goal may require large investments in product development, marketing, expansion, acquisitions, and organizational growth to help the venture keep its edge over direct competitors. eBay was started by Pierre Omidyar with a business model that focused on online auctions. He was able to build the venture to about $250,000 in monthly sales without any outside equity. But when better-funded competitors came along, Omidyar was forced to seek venture capital to stay in the lead. Along with capital, the VCs also brought in a professional CEO named Margaret Whitman.

VCs Fund Ventures that Are Growing Rapidly Despite Negative Cash Flow

VCs like to invest in potentially dominant ventures in emerging industries and want the venture to grow fast to dominate its industry. VCs accept negative cash flows to keep growing. They also fund the cash-flow deficit in return for additional equity. Some of the poster children using this formula include WeWork and Uber. Unfortunately for WeWork, the funding spigot stopped before Adam Neumann anticipated. Uber is scrambling to turn around its cash flow.

How Finance-Smart Entrepreneurs Take Off

Most billion-dollar entrepreneurs launched their business with limited cash and positive cash flow.

The capital-dependent VC method requires lots of cash that is normally obtained in stages.

The capital-smart method is to launch and grow with limited amounts of cash and to make sure you never run out of cash. This requires finance-smart coordination, including ensuring the right timing, growth rate, sales and marketing strategies, operations strategies, management strategies, and resource strategies.

Finance-smart, high-performance entrepreneurs take off without capital for a variety of reasons: Either they do not need VC to grow, they are not in industries attractive to VCs, or they do not want to cede control to the VCs.

Perhaps most importantly, they do not qualify for VC in early stages since their unique differentiation is dependent on the skills of the entrepreneur and not the uniqueness of their opportunity.

Billion-dollar entrepreneurs acquire the right skills. In addition to the functional expertise, if they are in emerging industries such as programming for Zuckerberg or cooking for Ells, or have industry experience in an existing industry, like Dick Schulze and Amancio Ortega, the most important business skills acquired by these entrepreneurs are sales/ marketing and financial management. They are accountants who knew how to sell value.

Finance-smart entrepreneurs control and take off. To do this, they use the following strategies:

- 💰 Focus to dominate with less
- 💰 Sell direct and own the market
- 💰 Pace to lead the industry
- 💰 Adjust to take off with limited cash

Chapter 15

Focus to Dominate with Less

At the start, ventures have few resources. Getting more can
be very expensive. In addition to capital, the key resources
that are always in limited supply are management time,
skills, and attention. Focus is critical.

Should you diversify or focus? If you should focus, where? A key
decision that a start-up needs to make is whether to focus on one
market segment and dominate it, or to diversify and "hedge" its
risks by entering multiple product-segment combinations. If you
should diversify, when, where, and how should you do it? This
decision has key financial and competitive implications.

In addition to poor management—which is the root cause of all
business failures, since management makes and implements all
decisions—one of the other major reasons for business failure is
not focusing on the right product-segment combination.

Highly successful ventures are usually the most dominant
companies in their direct competitive group. Ventures that do
not dominate their market and industry are at a competitive
disadvantage vis-a-vis the group leader. To dominate a segment,

ventures need to best satisfy the needs of that segment, or risk losing to those who do focus on those needs and become the most competitive company in that segment. New and emerging companies, and often even existing ones, cannot be all things to all customers.

Jack Welch's rule for GE was that each business should be a leader in its market. He noted that even large businesses should focus and do one thing well because "you cannot be everything to everybody."[88]

Why Focus?

Most seasoned venture financiers would suggest focusing on one product and one segment at the start. After the venture takes off and succeeds in one product-market combination, it can then find cheaper money to expand into other markets or add more products. This strategy can be counter intuitive especially because many entrepreneurs think they can reduce risk by diversifying as they may have learned in finance class.

The key difference between financiers and entrepreneurs is that financiers don't manage their investments on a full-time basis. A financial portfolio is more passive than a venture, although it does take time to find the right investments, negotiate the deal, and monitor the ventures, and results are dependent on the performance of the investments in the portfolio. Diversification allows financiers to spread their risks over many investments because some will fail.

Entrepreneurship is a hands-on activity, and as an entrepreneur, you are an active manager with limited financial, human, or other resources. If you decide to diversify your risk by operating in, say, two market segments, some competitors could focus on one segment and win there. Other competitors could focus on the other segment and win there. You may be able to win in multiple segments if you are supremely qualified, like an Elon Musk, but what are the odds? And do you want to gamble in multiple segments? You may diversify yourself out of business.

Herb Kelleher founded Southwest Airlines and made it into one of the most profitable airlines in the airline business. As Kelleher put it, airlines move in for the kill as soon as they sense weakness in a competitor. Kelleher focused on the airline industry. As he notes, "We don't know everything about everything. We know about one thing."[89]

The key reason to focus is to dominate. To become dominant, nearly all of Minnesota's high-performance entrepreneurs focused on one product and one segment until they dominated the segment. Then they expanded into new segments using the initial product or moved into new products to serve their existing segment and become stronger there. Diversification into unrelated product-segment combinations are considered riskier. This strategy was first noted by Igor Ansoff, one of the first great thinkers in management theory.

Focus Can Get the Best Customers

Successful entrepreneurs focus on the right customers. Trying to market and sell a new product to many segments, each with its own unmet needs and marketing challenges, could diffuse the company's efforts and lead to failure. Entrepreneurs who seek to sell to anyone and everyone without a focused plan are unlikely to be taken seriously by professional investors. Investors realize how difficult it is to reach and convince large numbers of people to buy anything, especially from a new company.

To focus on the right customers, entrepreneurs should understand the market segments. Grouping customers into market segments helps entrepreneurs focus their product, marketing, sales, pricing, operations, and financing strategies on the right segment. In addition to dominating the right segment, the venture could grow fast if the segment is fast growing.

What if some of your potential customers who want to buy from you are not in your target segment? How does this affect your business? Ask yourself a few questions before you change your focus:

- Will you incur additional expenses to serve them?
- Will you take on more risks?
- Do you have to make changes to your business?
- Does this take you away from your central focus?
- Is this new segment attractive? Is it more attractive than the one you originally selected?

Note that you may not succeed if you don't dominate the selected segment, and you will not have the resources to dominate more than one segment at the start.

When Craig Swanson and his partner were building Definity Health, they decided to focus on large, self-insured employers for their point of entry. Definity developed the Health Reimbursement Account (HRA) as an employee benefit and to cut health costs. The HRA combined aspects of the medical savings account with insurance above a defined limited, include consumer tools to inform and select the right type of care, and include the right network of care providers. Definity did not want to carry the risk of selling insurance, and large, self-insured employers have a strong incentive to keep their employees happy and save money doing so.

Focus Allows Optimal Use of Limited Resources

Your cost of money is very high at the start, and the availability is low. Initially, your cost of equity could be as high as 80 percent to 100 percent per year, especially if you are seeking funding from professional investors. As the venture grows and becomes less risky, your cost of professional VC can decrease to around 30 percent at later stages.

This high cost of VC at the early stages means that ventures should focus and dominate the first market before diversifying to other product-segment combinations. Focusing on multiple product-segment combinations will force the venture to raise larger quantities of expensive money at the start and allocate scarce resources among multiple product-market combinations. Investing in two products or two markets at this stage means that the venture is paying a high financing price for two businesses. Should the venture raise more money at this stage, assuming it is available, and dilute the founders, or should it dominate one segment and then expand into other segments with lower-cost money?

Along with limited money, leadership time is scarce, and management may be inexperienced. It is usually smarter to focus on dominating the target market, then expand to others when the cost of money is much lower and the company can attract high-caliber managers.

Focus Can Beat "First Mover" for Growth

Very few first movers win. Actually, only 11 percent of first movers dominated their segment.[90] To win as the first mover, you have to build an insurmountable lead, or do everything correctly. Otherwise, followers can analyze your strategy, improve on your product or service—maybe with more money since capital flows to emerging markets after the opportunity has been identified—

and win. So, if you focus on the right segment and dominate, others may not be able to dislodge you.

After making his rural stores dominant in Arkansas, Sam Walton of Walmart was able to use his strong position there to dominate the rest of rural America and then the rest of country. He held off competitors like Kmart that tried to enter the rural market after Walmart had established its dominance. But Kmart was not able to break Walmart's stranglehold on the rural market.

Focus Can Help You Achieve Dominance

Settling for mediocrity never made anyone great. To win, you need to dominate. But it is tough for a venture to dominate a market unless it focuses on the specific needs of the key customer segment and develops and implements a strategy to serve those unmet needs better than competitors. So understand how to dominate your target market by leveraging your unique advantage.

Horst Rechelbacher built Aveda by focusing on a unique and exclusive distribution system. He already had built a network by training beauticians in his schools. He helped them become distributors and developed his organic-products business. These students who had already been trained by Rechelbacher in his techniques were able to use and thereby promote his products optimally.

- Rechelbacher had learned the benefits of vertical integration by observing a business in India with proprietary products that were made in its own factories and sold using in its own stores. This vertical integration gave the company control over all aspects—and an advantage over its competitors.

- Using this model, Rechelbacher helped his best salespeople become his exclusive distributors and his former beautician students to sell his products. This allowed him to control the entire sales and distribution function. He sold to the top tier of consumers who valued him and were willing to pay more. He did not worry about growth. He worried about the customer experience and made his exclusive distributors worry about customers.

💰 To create his own retail brand, Rechelbacher started his store in a high-traffic location on Madison Avenue and designed it for optimum visibility. At his second store in Soho, he did better than expected. Having seen the success of Rechelbacher's own stores in Manhattan, his distributors were clamoring to get in on the retail and education area of the business. Since his distributors sold his product exclusively, he helped them open beauty schools and stores in locations with the best visibility to target customers.

💰 Aveda claimed to be the only company in the salon industry with proprietary products, a training center for hair designers, and proprietary mass-distribution infrastructure. When he sold the business to Estee Lauder for $300 million, Rechelbacher had 15 beauty schools and about 250 stores.

Steve Shank of Capella realized that no one had mastered the use of the Internet for education because of its newness. To minimize potential problems, Shank decided to work with students who had successfully obtained an undergraduate university degree. He decided that Capella would focus on offering graduate degrees. This was smart because the dominant company in the field, the University of Phoenix, was strong in undergraduate education but not in graduate programs. But focusing on graduate education also meant that the students would demand a higher level of quality and competence from their teachers, so

Capella would have to offer a high-quality product to differentiate itself from the others. By focusing on graduate programs, adding a high-quality, university-like education with the efficiency of a business, with a commitment to quality, service, and respect, Shank built a leader in long-distance education.

Conclusion

Focus your business on your competitive advantage. As an entrepreneur, you have limited resources and limited management capacity. Diversification is for later stages. By focusing, entrepreneurs are able to dominate their initial market by designing their products, services, marketing, and resources to make the customers in that segment happier and keep them for the long term. The key is to be wise about the right segment to focus on, i.e. the segment that will offer the fastest revenues and cash flow, and which segment will offer the best long-term advantage.

Dominating this initial segment can give you a strong base and cash flow to expand to other segments. Entrepreneurs who seek to diversify their business before they dominate one segment leave themselves vulnerable in all their segments. As noted earlier, Walton focused on rural America before expanding to other markets. Mark Zuckerberg focused on the nation's top-ranked universities before branching out to other universities and then to the rest of the world. Steve Jobs focused on the iPod before expanding to other iconic products such as the iPhone and the iPad. Bill Gates focused on making his operating system the standard for PCs before expanding to other products.

Entrepreneurs focus. Corporations diversify.

Chapter 16

Sell Direct to Connect with Your Market

Business without sales is like Hamlet without the prince.
—Joseph Schumpeter

Billion-dollar entrepreneurs focused on sales and marketing strategies that offered positive cash flow with capital efficiency and long-term control of the market. To do this, they had to find the right sales drivers to sell more with less, to keep more of the sales dollar, and to make their customers happier for long-term dominance. To make their customers happier, most of them sold direct to their customers. Selling direct also allowed them to control their rate of growth and the need for cash.

Sales do not just happen. Technology-oriented entrepreneurs who focus on developing the next great high-tech product sometimes assume that that their "great" product will sell itself. The odds are against it. Billion-dollar entrepreneurs know that sales don't just happen—they have to make it happen with minimal cost and do it quickly. These entrepreneurs have used various unique strategies to get sales.

Mary Kay Ash used diamonds, vacations, and pink Cadillac cars as sales force incentives to build Mary Kay Cosmetics into a powerhouse.

William Wrigley built his chewing gum empire by sending free chewing gum to people in the phone book when the telephone was just emerging, based on the assumption that if people could afford the phone, they could afford the gum.[91] Jeff Bezos hired mobile billboards to roam outside the stores of his giant competitor, Barnes & Noble, to entice customers to find the book they wanted at Amazon.com, his online store.[92] Roger Penske promoted his company, the Penske Auto Group, by entering cars into races in the race-car circuit, such as the Indianapolis 500, where his teams have won a record fifteen times. He noted that winning the Indy 500 gave him advertising exposure that he could never afford.[93] But not many can enter and win the Indy 500.

Steve Ells opened his first Chipotle next to the campus of the University of Denver in 1993 because his initial market was young college students who had been taught about the merits of organic food.[94]

Tilman Fertitta, the 100 percent owner of Landry's and one of the biggest restaurateurs in the US, notes that "if you go to the water, you can put an average seafood place next to the greatest steak house and people are going to eat seafood."[95]

When Michael Dell was a teenager, he found a job selling newspapers. He realized that people start subscribing to newspapers when they move or get married. So, he got the addresses of people applying for marriage licenses and sent them direct mail offers. He got thousands of customers.[96]

Sales drivers are your strategies to get sales. If you are a retail store located in a shopping center, your sales driver is mall traffic in front of your store, and the cost of your sales driver is the rent. Alternatively, if you are operating from your garage or basement where there is no traffic, your sales driver has to find and sell customers. In such a case, sales drivers can include advertising, direct mail, telemarketing, sales personnel, or using your own time to sell. The cost of your sales driver is the investment you make in the driver(s) you pick.

Sales drivers are important because startups need sales quickly and in sufficient amounts to make a profit and show positive cash flow. To get sales, ventures need the right sales driver to get the maximum amount of sales and margins in the shortest time to dominate their segment for the longest time with the least investment.

But knowing the right sales driver and the productivity of the sales driver in a start-up is a problem.

Two numbers in a start-up's pro-forma financial projections are always wrong and lead to missed projections. The first is sales, including the level of sales and the timing. The second equally important number is the cost to get sales. You may spend money on the wrong sales driver and not get the results you expected. Or, if you have the right sales driver, you may have to spend more than you planned, which may lead to failure because you run out of money before positive cash flow.

Existing businesses know the right mix and productivity of their sales drivers and how much they have to spend to get the desired level of sales. They have history. Their key issues are to improve the productivity of their sales drivers or adjust the mix, especially as new sales drivers like online marketing are developed.

New businesses do not have this advantage. They don't know what will sell, how to sell, or whom to target based on who will buy immediately and pay the highest price. This is one reason why many entrepreneurs change business models after they start. What may have worked for other direct or indirect competitors may not work for them because they are new. What may have worked previously may not work anymore due to changing habits, customs, customers, trends, technologies, or sales drivers. What may have worked in a previous job in a similar industry may not work in the new venture.

Experience may not work for a new venture for a variety of reasons: it faces entrenched competitors; customers may not switch for small benefits; the venture may need a new way to reach the market; and the venture may need more money and time due to skepticism.

Why Sell Direct?

HIGH-PERFORMANCE ENTREPRENEURS SELL DIRECT.
Sixty-eight percent of Minnesota's billion-dollar entrepreneurs picked the sales driver that allowed direct-to-customer sales (Figure 8). An additional seven percent developed and controlled proprietary, exclusive channels.

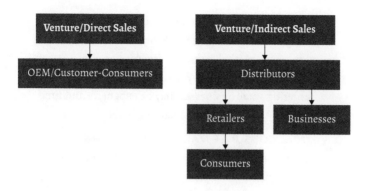

Figure 8. Direct vs. Indirect Selling

Sales channels and sales drivers influence costs, revenues, margins, and your connection to and "ownership" of the customer. When you sell via channels, the consumer's connection is with the business level that sells to the customer, such as the retailer. That can make it more difficult to build your relationship and your brand without expensive advertising, which costs money that emerging ventures do not have.

Both VCs and billion-dollar entrepreneurs have done well when they sell "direct to customers." A direct channel to the customer gives more control over sales and the distribution process, and importantly, offers a higher level of control over the customer relationship. Intermediaries, such as wholesalers, distributors, and retailers may offer the hope of high volume but they add complexity, may require discounts and incentives, and importantly, they control the relationship with the final consumer. However, if the end consumer will not buy directly from you, you may need intermediaries.

You can sell directly to markets:

- 💰 **BUSINESSES:** Businesses can include large Fortune 1000-type corporations that may not buy from new ventures. Targeting mid-sized businesses may be better for new ventures because there are more of them and they buy in larger quantities than small businesses. They are also more easily reachable than selling to consumers or small businesses and can help you diversify your customer base. Targeting small businesses may be expensive and time consuming, especially on a national level.

- Ⓢ **LOCAL CONSUMER MARKETS:** This can be done via the retail model with company stores or franchisees or through other means such as a sales force or local advertising.

- Ⓢ **NATIONAL NICHE MARKETS:** This can be attractive if there are media targeted to this group such as specialized media, websites, or media outlets that can be used for promotions.

- Ⓢ **NATIONAL MASS MARKETS:** Selling directly to a national consumer-focused mass market is usually difficult and expensive for undercapitalized new ventures. Although the Internet has made it possible for new ventures to reach national and global consumer markets, the cost to identify, reach, convince, sell, and service to such markets can be expensive and time consuming. VC has been prominent in the group of Internet-based companies that have targeted this market.

- Ⓢ **GOVERNMENTS:** The key problem with selling to governments is that they often value price or connections over value (a generalization that seems to be mostly true). This means that high-value products may not be recognized as such and may have to be sold at lower than desired prices.

Entrepreneurs can also sell indirectly to local or national markets through indirect channels such as using sales reps and distributors who sell to wholesalers and retailers. The key problem with this strategy is the large amount of money needed to build the channels, offer the discounts needed by the intermediaries, and invest in the marketing needed to convince consumers to select your product from the retailers' shelves.

If you have a choice between selling directly to your customers or selling indirectly to consumers via intermediaries, compare the skills to sell either way and the costs. Most importantly, remember that the customers have a direct relationship with the ultimate vendor, not with you.

Selling Direct Can Help You Focus on Segment Needs

Each customer segment has its own unique needs. Ventures will need to spend the cost and time to identify the right customers, reach them, sell value for the right price, and close the sale. Sales-driver effectiveness can vary based on the newness of the venture and the nature of the relationship between the customer and the venture.

It may be easy for a large well-known company to sell without an expensive marketing campaign, but a small company may need an expensive campaign to build credibility and establish credentials before customers will buy. A new venture selling to a large corporation may find that the purchasing agent prefers to work with established companies since it reduces the risks for both their company and their own careers.

New ventures need to target potential customers who are attracted to the innovation and are willing to take the risk of buying from unproven companies. These customers are often more likely to be pioneers who do not follow the crowd. But the problem is knowing who these pioneers and early-adopters are, how to reach them, and how to convince them that you are "cool."

After identifying the right segment, ventures need to find the right sales driver to reduce risk and the cost of sales while generating faster sales and cash flow. To do this, test alternatives.

When Brett Shockley started Spanlink, the first customer he tried to get was the *Star Tribune*, the major newspaper in the Twin Cities. Although Shockley's proposal was the most competitive and offered the highest benefits, the *Star Tribune's* committee in charge of making the decision did not want to work with Spanlink. They were not sure Spanlink would be in business in a year. Their preference was Wang Labs, which was liquidated a few years later. The executive responsible for the decision overruled the committee and hired Spanlink.[97]

Selling Direct Can Help You Get Started for Less when Money Is Expensive

Selling to large consumer markets via channels often has additional sales costs and unique problems. Besides the cost of developing the sales and distribution channels, there is the cost of filling the pipelines and the cost of convincing potential customers to buy the product.

Picking markets that you can reach directly rather than through complex channels may help you get started more easily and with a lower investment. Growth at the start may not be as fast, but it could help you get closer to your customers, satisfy their unmet needs, and reach profitability and cash flow.

When Kevin Plank started Under Armour, he initially sold to football teams. His under-uniform T-shirts were made with synthetic fabrics that did not absorb sweat like cotton T-shirts. To sell this message to the football teams, he sold directly to them by making cold calls all day and by shipping at night. His first sale in 1996 was to Georgia Tech. Today, he has Tom Brady of the Patriots as his supporter and shareholder.[98]

John Paul DeJoria, cofounder of John Paul Mitchell Systems, started his company by having a manufacturer make a sample run of his beauty products. The manufacturer gave him two weeks to pay for the order. In that time, DeJoria called on salons and received orders and payment from twelve customers. He also called on a distributor who agreed to carry the line. He paid the manufacturer on time.[99]

Selling direct to customers means that you don't have to invest the time or money to sell to the intermediaries such as wholesalers and retailers, pay slotting fees to the retailers, arrange for promotions at the retail locations, and then spend money on advertising to get consumers to pick up your product. This means that the initial cash and equity needed can be lower. At the start, money is very expensive and getting to positive cash flow can help raise expansion capital.

Jill Blashack Strahan of Tastefully Simple decided to sell gourmet foods via home parties because she could sell directly to consumers and it did not require marketing money she did not have or distribution channels she could not access. The home party was the ideal fit. It was scalable and she knew others who had built successful companies using home parties. She had attended a few home parties herself, and people, particularly women, seemed to enjoy them. When she started with home parties, some of the women attending the party bought her products. and some signed on as sales consultants to sell Tastefully Simple products. With a $6,000 investment, she has built a company with sales exceeding $140 million.[100]

EXAMPLE: The following example may help explain some pros and cons of direct selling. Assume that you can sell directly to consumers using the Internet or using intermediaries and a promotion campaign. The company that sells directly to the customer receives the full price (ten dollars in the example below minus the commissions). However, when it sells via intermediaries, it receives four dollars with the balance going to the retailer and distributor.

Option	A: Direct	B: Indirect
Price to consumer	$10	$10
Price to retailer	N/A	$5
Price to distributor (your price)	N/A	$4

Sales Costs:

Internet Advertising:	Cost of Ads	Promotion
Channel inventory:	None	Fill Channels

Regarding the costs:

💰 In the direct approach (A), the company bears the full cost of identifying the customers and selling to them. This is the key: if this is done effectively and at low cost, the venture could succeed.

💰 In the indirect method, the company may have media costs and in-store promotions. If the media campaign works, the venture may succeed. In the indirect approach, there is also the investment needed for inventory to fill the channels.

The key disadvantage with indirect sales is that the ultimate vendor is the one who has the direct relationship with the consumer—not your company. Can the vendor switch from you to another supplier, or can you build a strong enough relationship with the consumer that the retailer *has* to carry your product?

What is the cost to build this brand loyalty? The benefit of selling indirectly is that you may be in more outlets more quickly. But then, you also need more capital.

So evaluate your options carefully to see if you need a coordinated campaign to sell via channels, or whether the company is better off with a direct-to-consumer business model and marketing campaign.

When Rechelbacher of Aveda started selling beauty products on a national level, he realized that the distributors were selling many competing products and did not adequately highlight the uniqueness of Aveda's products. As he put it, "I did not want to be number thirty-six, the last one they sold." He took the best sales people from his own organization and helped them become his exclusive distributors so he could control the entire sales and distribution function to ensure that they targeted the right markets and followed the right strategies and practices. Rechelbacher wanted to focus on high-end customers who valued him and were willing to pay more. He increased his share in his target salons from 5 percent of retail sales to 30 percent of retail sales by designing his products, training the hair dressers, and offering the services to keep them happy. Rechelbacher did not worry about growth. He worried about the customer experience and made sure that his exclusive distributors worried about the same thing. They became very successful and made him even more so.

Selling Direct Helps You to Own the Relationship

When asked, nearly all the billion-dollar entrepreneurs who were selling direct to consumers noted that they preferred this method, which helped them stay close to their customers. Selling direct helped them understand and meet their customers' needs.

Selling direct helps entrepreneurs "own" the relationship and offer better service, feedback, and margins without the upfront channel-building costs. Billion-dollar entrepreneurs knew how to sell value directly to their customers and earn high-income margins while keeping their costs low.

Even leading high-tech entrepreneurs need to do this. Earl Bakken of Medtronic who invented the electronic cardiac pacemaker realized that he needed to sell to the physicians who controlled the sale and not just depend on the unique medical benefits of their product. Bakken and his partner got out of their comfort zone and learned to do so.[101]

This means that if you have a choice between selling directly to your customers or selling indirectly via intermediaries such as wholesalers or retailers, know that the customers are not yours, but the intermediary's when you sell via channels. You can build a brand, but how much will that cost you in advertising? By selling direct, you own the relationship, and it is usually easier to keep a direct relationship alive. Therefore, direct sales are usually preferred by billion-dollar entrepreneurs, especially at the start of the business.

Jeremy Stoppelman of Yelp notes that one of the benefits of his direct marketing strategy was that he is not reliant on Google's searches. Since Google competes with him on local advertising, his dependence on Google for revenues could have handicapped him. By having a direct connection, he does not have to pay Google, nor can they hurt him as much.[102]

When Gustavo Cisneros of the Cisneros Group inherited his father's business, which was primarily in Pepsi and related industries, he continued his father's policy of vertical integration. Cisneros went into the grocery-retail business and started a TV station. This way, he could promote his products in his own stores and via his own media channels and own the customers.

One danger of this policy is that you may be competing with your customers, and they may not want to carry your products. Cisneros avoided this problem by offering high-demand brands that other retailers wanted to carry.[103]

Direct Selling Connects You to Customers

Accessibility to customers is one of the major challenges facing new and expanding ventures. Customers are not always open to new ideas and new vendors unless they perceive strong benefits, acceptable risks, and competitive costs. But the cost to reach customers, convince them to buy, and be able to service the sale can be very high.

When Tony Hsieh took over Zappos,[104] drop-shipment, i.e. direct shipment from the shoe manufacturer to the customer, was about 25 percent of the business. Zappos eliminated this portion of the business because the company could not distinguish itself among its customers and own the market without controlling the inventory and the customer. Hsieh noted that they *"had to give up the easy money, manage the inventory, and take the risk."* To build a brand around customer service, they had to be able to deliver it. A few years later, Zappos was sold to Amazon.com for gazillions.

Dan Gilbert, along with his brother and a friend, started Rock Financial, which was later sold to Intuit, became Quicken Loans, and was then bought back by Dan Gilbert, who retained the name. But instead of following most mortgage bankers who relied on real-estate brokers for their leads, Gilbert and his partners decided to sell mortgages directly by using 1-800 numbers and a call center. It was only a short step from there to online sales and marketing when the Internet was introduced. They sold the company to Intuit for $532 million and repurchased it for $65 million.[105]

Initial growth for entrepreneurs is usually slower when selling directly, but you control the channels and it gives you the potential to improve customer relationships and adjust to fit customer needs.

Direct Selling Allows Easier Bottom-Up Financial Analysis to Reduce Risk

When forecasting the finance needs of new and growing ventures, it helps to know the relationship between the sales strategy, revenues, costs, and financial needs.

A "top-down" approach examines the size of the market and then assumes a market share that is supposed to be "reasonable." Corporations with experience can use this method with reasonable accuracy because they already have a marketing strategy in place and a history of market share. Barring unforeseen circumstances or changed trends, corporations expect to produce similar results in the future. New companies, on the other hand, cannot extrapolate from the past since there is no history, no knowledge of the right media, and no understanding of the connection between the media mix, investment, and number of customers or the average sales per customer. All these assumptions will have to be made from the bottom up.

A "bottom-up" approach starts with the actual level of resources spent on each sales driver to generate the desired level of customer impressions such as traffic counts or advertising. Next comes forecasting of prospects, orders, and sales based on the productivity of the specific sales driver(s) used. The more detailed the assumptions made at this stage, and the clearer the rationale for these assumptions, the better the company will be in developing realistic marketing budgets and projecting realistic sales levels.

By tracking the results from the sales-driver tests, the company can determine its most productive allocation of funds for marketing, the level and cost of marketing support needed, and forecast potential sales. It can incorporate these numbers into its projections to estimate the level of financing needed. The venture can then monitor the actual results to see if any changes are warranted as the company embarks on its growth and observe how these changes affect the level of cash needed.

Guthy-Renker has become a billion-dollar company ($1.5 billion+ in sales and a valuation of nearly $3 billion[106]) by knowing which sales drivers were productive in its infomercial business. The company got its start by buying airtime for its thirty-minute infomercials, which included an 800 number. It used up to 10,000 800 numbers at one time. However, with the growth of mobile phones and the Internet, the company is struggling to know where its customers are coming from and how they are finding out about products. At one time, the company knew the source of its orders. Now, it is wondering "Why? How? Who?"

Selling Direct Can Get Higher Margins but with Higher Initial Cost

When selling via channels, each of the layers in the channel wants a discount. When selling direct, the venture gets to keep the entire sales dollar. However, the key question is whether this extra margin makes up for the additional marketing expenses that are likely to be incurred to sell direct-to-the-customer and to service the customer. If you can find a way to market directly for less money, do it.

Jill Blashack Strahan built Tastefully Simple by realizing that at parties where she sold products, some of the customers wanted to organize their own parties to sell, which expanded her marketing network. This was the ideal marketing strategy—

where you get paid to sell. She built her business to more than
$140 million in sales.

Selling Direct Can Differentiate Your Business

If your products are very similar to your competitors, and the
other companies are established companies, customers may not
buy from you, and investors are unlikely to want to invest in a
"me-too" company. One way to differentiate your company would
be to find a new way to sell, especially when new sales-driver
technologies are emerging and affordable.

Amazon.com found a new way to sell books directly to customers.
Dell found a way to sell PCs directly to customers. Both destroyed
many competitors and became giants. The Internet continues to
destroy old business models.

Selling Direct Can Reduce Returns and Increase Certainty

Direct sales are usually preferred by billion-dollar entrepreneurs,
especially at the start of the business, and with good reason.
When products do not sell at the retail level, dealers usually
return them. This means that the risk is borne by you, the
entrepreneur, and not by the dealers, especially if they are given
extended terms to pay.

Joel Ronning, who built Digital River into a giant, was a product
manager with Remington Rand where he was managing
peripheral products for the Mac computer. When Remington
Rand was sold, Ronning was able to buy the Mac peripheral-
products business. He formed a company called Mirror
Technologies, hired engineers, and expanded the line to include
other peripheral products. He sold directly to consumers and
to small businesses via newspaper and computer magazine ads
and indirectly via computer dealers. He found that direct was
better: the cash flow was much better and more than made up

for the increased advertising expenses. When he sold indirectly via dealers, he had problems with payments and returns. The dealers would return unsold goods after a few months if they were unable to sell, thus transferring the risk of unsold products to the company.

Conclusion

When possible, pick markets that you can reach directly rather than indirectly through intermediaries. Form alliances with established corporations to reach more difficult segments, such as national and international markets, consumer markets, small-business markets or customers who may not buy from new businesses. Focus on the segment from "heaven"—those who can be reached directly, buy instantly, pay quickly, value highly and are prestigious, growing, and in potentially large numbers. When possible, sell directly to customers who will pre-pay. Picking the right sales strategy can be the most important decision you will make.

Chapter 17

Pace to Lead the Industry

Investing heavily before your customers are ready to buy or after your direct competitors have taken off could mean that others get an advantage and dominate your market. To lead your industry, you need to account for three speeds: the speed allowed by your cash and cash flow, the speed of your market, and the speed of your competitors. To lead the industry, you need to grow along with your customers and your cash flow faster than the industry. This is not easy.

Pacing is crucial. Grow too fast and you may run out of cash. Grow slowly and you could be beaten by fast-growing competitors. Growth is a complex issue. Some key growth-related questions are how to grow, how fast to grow, and how to finance the growth.

The key *external* factors behind the right growth rate are the speed of the market, i.e. the customer's willingness to switch to a new industry or to your new venture, and the growth rate of your direct competitors. Spending too much money to grow before the customer is ready can waste valuable resources. Not growing as fast as your direct competitors when the market is willing could mean a loss of market share and leads to failure.

The key *internal* factors are cash flow and cash availability. Seeking to increase cash flow by increasing prices could stifle current growth. Seeking to increase it by cutting expenses may slow future growth. Seeking external financing to sustain the growth rate could result in a loss of control. Not seeking it could affect your growth.

To succeed, you need to balance all these factors.

Why Grow at the Right Speeds?

To Survive the Lean Years

Timing is everything. Don't drink wine before its time. Don't try to push a service when the customer is not ready. Customers do not show up just because you have opened your doors. Sales of new products and services often grow in the shape of a hockey stick. Sales are slow to ramp up initially, and more money spent on marketing may be wasted. *When the market is ready, it takes off.* This means that you need to keep your gunpowder dry till the market is ready to grow and invest when it starts to take off. The time from start-up till take off takes at least three years, and most times, it takes longer.[107] So you need to stay lean, patient, and persistent.

When a recession hit the temporary-staffing industry, Tim Doherty of Doherty Employment began to look for a new growth strategy. He had been keeping track of a new industry trend which was then called employee leasing. There were a number of synergies between this new service and his existing temporary-staffing service. For many of his smaller clients, this meant a large reduction in paperwork, human resources administration and resulting overhead. To implement this new strategy, Doherty started Doherty Employer Services, a Human Resource Outsourcing organization. In addition to hiring a staff of HR and benefits professionals, Doherty hired salespeople experienced in selling outsourcing services. But the HR outsourcing service was new in the Twin Cities, and Minnesota companies were reluctant to outsource HR. Doherty initially lost a "boatload of money" for trying to sell a service before its time. By cutting expenses and changing his business-marketing philosophy to a more realistic, less costly, and less aggressive approach, Doherty returned to profitability.

Customers Need Time to Understand Benefits and Risks

Customers usually don't want to take risks—unless the benefits are commensurate. This suggests that entrepreneurs should give customers the time and opportunity to test and try their products and services. Customers, especially large corporations, take time to adopt new ways, and only if there are compelling reasons to do so from a financial, business, and risk perspective. Some of the factors that influence the rate of adoption of new products include the product's or service's cost, benefits, and risks; ease of understanding the benefits and usage; and whether it can be tested.

Brett Shockley of Spanlink developed products in the telecom field that were sometimes too far ahead of the market. An example was WebCall, the app that let consumers click a button on the website to reach a call center agent. The problem was that adding this solution required several corporate departments, including information technology, to work together, which they had not done previously. At Merrill Lynch, twenty-five people crowded the room at the first meeting, all introducing themselves to each other. Shockley realized that he would not get a quick sale.

Avoid Being Left behind as the Industry Takes Off

Emerging industries are slow to take off. But when the inflexion point arrives and the industry starts to take off, you need to be aware, alert, and ready. Once you lag behind competitors, it's hard to catch up. In addition, your operations and financing need to be in control so that your cash flow and profits don't suffer as you are expanding.

But don't add overhead before it's time. One of the most difficult decisions in expansion is knowing when to add overhead. The business world is littered with entrepreneurs and executives who expanded, added cost and infrastructure, and then found that their customers were not ready or their competitive advantage had faded. The additional overhead often destroyed their company. So, make sure that you can sustain your sales and margins to pay for the added overhead.

The retail food industry has an annual convention in Chicago when meat buyers get together to discuss innovations and trends. The meat buyer for Kroger's was the keynote speaker on trends and innovations in the retail meat business. He talked about Lloyd Sigel's products (Lloyd's Barbeque). The first slide he showed to the country's meat buyers was his entire meat case filled with Lloyd's products. Lloyd's phones started ringing off the hook. Sales took off and the company could not satisfy demand. Ribs went from being a hard-to-sell meat product to the hot meat product. Lloyd's expanded rapidly by renting meat plants in Fridley (Minnesota), Klemme (Iowa), and Newport (Minnesota). Sigel did not expand based on hope. He did it after demand showed up.

But competitors may dominate if they have more resources and can grow faster. So, consider getting VC if competitors have corporate alliances, have raised VC, are likely to get VC from Silicon Valley VC funds, or if you can seek an advantage with VC from Silicon Valley VC funds.

eBay was growing rapidly when founder Pierre Omidyar sought venture capital to dominate his industry. Others were also entering the market, and Omidyar realized that he needed to dominate this emerging industry if he was to succeed. He had to be the one who grew the fastest and got the most customers and vendors to dominate in Internet auctions. With venture capital, eBay dominated the industry.

Watch for Slowing Growth

If your core business is maturing, you may want to expand to other growth opportunities in related areas where you can apply your core competence and continue your growth. You may also want to capitalize on the business you have built and sell it, if that is your goal, when the market still values it highly.

The market kept growing and so did Bonnie Baskin's ViroMed. With overnight delivery becoming common, customers could be anywhere in the US. A pioneer in molecular diagnostics and genetic analysis, ViroMed grew to annual sales of $25 million and was highly profitable by the fall of 2000. Baskin also realized that creating and building the business was a "high" for her, personally, but managing was not as interesting. By 2000, the high-end clinical testing portion of the business had reached maturity, while the industrial testing part was still emerging and growing. So, Baskin decided to sell the clinical portion of ViroMed, and spun off the industrial testing into a new business called AppTec.

Conclusion

Forecasting your company's growth rate and planning for it is a difficult but important decision. You need to balance the speed of your cash and cash flow, the speed of your competitors, and the speed of your customers.

Chapter 18

Adjust to Takeoff with Limited Cash

There are "two kinds of forecasters: the ones who don't know and the ones who don't know they don't know."

—John Kenneth Galbraith[108]

Forecasting accurately is difficult, especially in start-up or emerging ventures. Knowing that forecasts can be wrong, entrepreneurs should be prepared to adjust. This means not betting the farm in one direction—until the direction is proven by the market. Unless, of course, you are willing to lose.

Flexibility is crucial in emerging industries and emerging ventures. Many billion-dollar entrepreneurs changed the direction of their ventures as the industry unfolded. Entrepreneurs in an emerging industry do not clearly see its challenges and opportunities at the start. To succeed:

💰 **ENTREPRENEURS TEST AND ADJUST:** Sam Walton tested various retail growth strategies for twelve years before he found the right one to build a big business. He found his opportunity when the big-box store concept was adopted by American retailers. Walton focused on big boxes in rural America.

- 💰 **ENTREPRENEURS FIND NEW WEDGE OPPORTUNITIES:** Entrepreneurs, even in an emerging industry, are competing with legacy industries and corporations, and all are looking for the weapon that will give them the edge. After starting a software company, Bill Gates found his edge by licensing the MS-DOS operating system to IBM and making it the standard for PCs.

- 💰 **ENTREPRENEURS FIND BETTER BUSINESS MODELS:** Taxicabs were a licensed, protected industry. Travis Kalanick changed Uber from a limo rental service to a taxi-without-cabs service and changed the industry beyond recognition.

Being able to accurately foretell the future would greatly help us take advantage of opportunities and minimize the risks of disasters. But predicting accurately is the domain of the Delphic oracles and astrologers. Mere mortals, including most entrepreneurs, make errors in their forecasts.

Existing corporations can use historical data and trend extrapolation to forecast. But as trends change, these forecasts fail. New ventures have no history to analyze or trends to project. This means that when initial venture plans work out, it is only due to rare good luck. Essentially, you want to establish a profitable relationship with your customers and dominate your market while your competitors seek to do the same. And until you start your business, you often do not know what or how well anything will work.

So you may have to adjust as opportunities and strategies unfold. That is why your initial business plan should not be sacred. 99.9 percent of the time, your forecasts will not be accurate. The industry changes. Customers change. The technology changes. You need to change and stay flexible.

Why Should You Stay Flexible?

The Market Will Not Adjust to You

Unless your initial product can be profitably marketed, immediately understood, embraced by customers, easily promoted with credibility, one-of-a-kind, and satisfies customers' unmet needs, the market will not adjust to you. You will have to adjust to the opportunity. Entrepreneurs may try to reduce this risk, but the reality of a new business is that customers have to change their habits and/or their vendors. The timing and nature of this shift is very difficult to predict, which means that most forecasts will be too optimistic and most strategies will miss the mark. So stay flexible and adjust to the reality that unfolds.

Glen Taylor built Taylor Corporation into a giant in the wedding invitation card industry by understanding the market and adjusting to its unmet needs. He was a leader in introducing wedding invitation cards based on the hot movies and songs of the day rather than using solely religious themes. He added the hot colors of the day for his cards based on changing fashions in wedding dresses. He made it easier to buy and receive the cards by adjusting his presses for faster delivery and by using UPS for guaranteed delivery. The market responded well.

Strategy Development Is Not a Straight Line

Note that new unproven businesses do not perform logically or predictably. There will always be something that does not work as you expected and which will have to be adjusted. Successful entrepreneurs such as Bill Gates, Sam Walton, and Dick Schulze have all improvised as they have grown. Earl Bakken started Medtronic to sell and service others' medical devices. But he found his ticket to dominance when he developed the heart pacemaker. By doing so, he started the medical electronics industry. Highly successful entrepreneurs followed their own strengths to develop their business opportunities. But then they took real feedback from the market and adjusted. Adjusting is one of the most difficult aspects of new-business development because you may have to make changes. Treat your plan as a guide to understand when to adjust.

As Richard Burke, founder of UnitedHealth, noted, a business plan is only what one starts with. Anticipate changing and refining it to dominate. But be aware of the difference between short-term needs to survive and long-term objectives. After his first alliance with a medical group was profitable, Burke bought out his investor/partner to seek other opportunities. Burke frequently had to look for revenue sources outside his primary business until the core business matured. For example, his data-processing staff found medical-transcription customers which helped the company meet payroll for almost a year.[109] But he stuck to his vision and built UnitedHealth.

Committing to a Direction before Aha Is Risky

Even if you are committed to one industry, test various models to find the right one for you. The first one may not be the best. In an emerging industry, the rules may not have been written and many emerging ventures may be jockeying for a position to find the right business strategy to dominate. In an established oligopolistic industry, entry may be difficult unless you use a new trend to grow and finding the right model in this new trend may need some testing. In an established fragmented industry, entry may be easy, but getting an edge may be difficult. Test options before committing to the one that is right for you and your venture.

When Jill Blashack Strahan of Tastefully Simple decided to start her first gift business, she took a business planning class at the area technical college and started to sell gift baskets out of her home. Then, she rented a kiosk at the local mall during the holidays. As her business grew and she could afford it, she started a storefront and lived in the back of the store.

Strahan experimented and found that creativity in names, themes, and designs had a strong influence on sales. She joined the local Holiday Crafter's Tour and offered six gift-basket themes and seven of her best easy-to-prepare food products. She repeated the Holiday Crafter's Tour for a second year and sold out again. This is when she had the big "Aha" for Tastefully Simple.

Based on the two Holiday Crafter's tours, she knew **what** she wanted to sell. But she did not know **how** to sell them until she read about a company that had succeeded selling household items through home parties. She connected the dots between her products, the sales strategy, her skills, and her passion. She knew that everything about the concept fit. She had tested her affordable indulgences in Alexandria, Minnesota, where her products had sold out at the Holiday Crafter's Tour. Most importantly, the feedback was real. Customers had proved it by buying her products—twice. *The idea of home parties appealed to her because she could sell directly to consumers and it did not require marketing money she did not have or distribution channels she could not access.* The home-party strategy was scalable, and she had read of others who had built very successful companies using home parties. She launched her company to great success.

Reality May Differ from Expectations

When reality is different from expectations, adjust. For a start-up, reality will always be different than expectations. Often, the difference is in the timing. Industries do not take off when you expect them to. In emerging industries and trends, you will also be faced with constantly changing conditions, with new impact, new competitors, new markets, and new strategies. Evaluate the trends in the market and how customers are behaving. Evaluate the reality of the industry and competitors' strengths and weaknesses. Then, pick the right strategy for you and constantly adjust until you find the one that helps you dominate.

When Tom Auth joined ITI after it had developed its product, the cost of residential security alarms was high, and the penetration rate was low. ITI's wireless alarms lowered the time and cost of installation for the dealers, giving the company a competitive edge. Auth took advantage of this benefit and of the low penetration rate of the wireless industry to grow organically without acquisitions. But with his next venture, Vomela, Auth faced a mature industry. There were many competitors and most of them were small, undercapitalized, and in need of management help. Auth decided to buy these companies and consolidate the industry, especially if he could buy at the right price. In ten years, he bought six companies with $34 million in annual sales and built Vomela from $3 million in sales to $81 million.

Times Change, and so Should You

Change is a constant. Just because a strategy helped you reach your current status does not mean that it will keep you successful. As industries and markets change, successful entrepreneurs also adjust. *Constantly track the market and its changes. Then, stay one step ahead.*

As the company grew, Dick Schulze realized that Best Buy was alone in the superstore format in the Upper Midwest. He found no obstacles to growth as he ploughed over his competitors. He had positioned himself well for growth. But now, he was competing with the giants of the industry such as Circuit City and Highland Superstores, and giant retailers like Sears and Montgomery Ward. They were moving into Best Buy's markets, including St. Louis, Minneapolis, and Milwaukee. The competitors were copying Best Buy's advertising and its branded products. This meant that Best Buy had to better position itself with the consumer. To counter this threat, Schulze developed the Concept II store, which looked more like a warehouse. The display was termed a "mass market display" with the actual boxes on the showroom floor. There was no pickup dock. Consumers just picked up the box from the showroom floor. Some vendors did not like the format and refused to sell their products to Best Buy.

Perhaps the most important innovation of Concept II store was the elimination of sales commissions. Schulze learned that with the warehouse-showroom concept, consumers could pick the right products with a lot less help, especially from high-value salespeople. He eliminated sales commissions and put his salespeople on a base salary, while still offering a bonus for storewide and companywide performance. This helped to convince customers that they would not be subject to high-pressure sales and employees that good performance would be rewarded. The new format succeeded.

Customers Want More Happiness

Customers always seek the highest value in terms of benefits and cost. So, you will need to adjust to business and business-model changes that can affect customer expectations and unmet needs caused by new technologies, competitors, and trends. Adjust to customers' needs, especially when they are unhappy.

In his first year, one of Tim Doherty's (Doherty Employment) clients, a meat packer, was working through the Thanksgiving weekend. When Doherty returned after the holiday weekend, he found a nasty message on his answering machine reminding him that his customers were open and had needs. The client fired Doherty over the phone. Doherty learned the hard way that it pays to learn about clients' needs and hours. He made sure that his offices were open and his phones were answered whenever his clients' operations were open.

Adjust to Fail Small, Win Big

A start-up involves many assumptions. Most of them will be wrong. The most important ones are about the level and timing of sales and the cost of sales and marketing. There are too many uncertainties that affect these variables. The basic problem is that no one knows your company, and customers are often reluctant to switch to new vendors and ventures, except in some industries such as food, where consumers often like to try out new items.

Lloyd Sigel built Lloyd's BBQ into a giant in cooked ribs. Since Lloyd's was the first mover, there were no direct competitors to benchmark against. So Sigel conducted tests to find out what customers would pay. He sold his products at different price points and personally called on the key retailers in the country to check the rate of sales. Customers' reactions allowed him to determine the right retail price point.

Sigel used the same test-based approach to find the right packaging for his product. He did not waste money on expensive market research, nor did he believe in the "sample size of one"—*I like it, therefore everyone will like it*—entrepreneurial approach. Sigel had his artist prepare multiple labels to prepare packages and left them on the lunchroom table. The packages that were popular with employees became his package. It was cost effective and market based.

Conclusion

Read the future correctly, and you can succeed. Read it incorrectly, and you could be a footnote in history. Since projections for startups are wrong, it pays to be flexible. Monitor the business and compare your reality with the projections. As a military advisor noted, *"when a map differs from the terrain, go with the terrain."* That's how you win a war. Do the same with emerging ventures to capture your venture's potential.

Part IV
Conclusion

Chapter 19

The Right Model for You

You can use one of two venture-development models to build your business.

THE OPPORTUNITY-BASED MODEL focuses on the idea, the plan, the technology, and the strategy. Entrepreneurs using this model develop the plan, seek financing, and then launch the business. If they get VC before they reach leadership Aha, the VCs recruit a professional CEO.

THE ENTREPRENEUR-BASED MODEL focuses on the skills of the entrepreneur. In this model, entrepreneurs develop the right skills, exploit their passion, develop their opportunity, find the right strategy based on market feedback, adjust to the unmet needs where they can get a long-term advantage, and take off without VC. After takeoff and after proving their leadership skills, they seek VC if their direct competitors have VC. Otherwise, they develop a capital-efficient model and grow without VC.

THE EXPERIENCE OF BILLION-DOLLAR ENTREPRENEURS suggests that entrepreneurs should consider delayed VC in Silicon Valley and avoid VC outside it. More than 90 percent of billion-dollar entrepreneurs outside Silicon Valley grew without VC. And more than 75 percent of those in Silicon Valley grew with delayed VC. They grew with skills. Billion-dollar entrepreneurs who avoided VC kept most of the wealth created, followed by those who delayed. Those who got VC early kept the least.

WHAT'S RIGHT FOR YOU? If you are seeking to build a high-potential venture in an emerging industry and can become more competitive with venture capital, you should consider getting it—after Aha. But either way, you always benefit from skills.

Afterword

I started Fastenal in 1967 with $31,000 from my savings and investments from four friends. I wanted to sell nuts and bolts using a vending machine.

A few weeks into the venture, I realized that the vending machine idea would not work. There were too many varieties of fasteners to fit into a vending machine. I "pivoted" and decided to open a retail store. We had about 10,000 competitors at the time. In time, we built Fastenal into the largest fastener company in the country with sales of more than five billion. We did this with no other external financing. We did have an IPO, but it was done more to allow our employees to purchase stock and share in the wealth they were creating, and to fund an educational foundation.

We grew with the skills and strategies noted in this book. Dr. Rao has done a wonderful job of analyzing my experience and that of many other unicorn-entrepreneurs in the US. And he has put together a book that everyone should read if they want to know how to build a growth venture, even a billion-dollar venture, and do it with internal cash flow and capital they control.

I know the world has changed since I started Fastenal and that there are more venture capitalists today. But as this book shows, very few entrepreneurs get venture capital, and even fewer succeed with it or gain from it. Your best option is to get the skills and use the smart strategies noted by Dr. Rao in this book. Good luck.

—**Bob Kierlin,** CEO and cofounder of Fastenal

Appendix

Table 6. Billion-Dollar Entrepreneur Net Worth Percent

Company	Name	Market Cap (bn)	Worth (bn)	Percent
Apple	Jobs	365	1.6	0.44
eBay	Omidyar	41	5.5	13
VC Early Ave.				7
Microsoft	Gates	218	82	38
Oracle	Ellison	146	32	22
Google	Page	188	17	9
Facebook	Zuckerberg	82	18	22
Salesforce.com	Benioff	18	1.8	10
Siebel Systems	Siebel	5.9	1.7	29
Intuit	Cook	16	1.2	8
PeopleSoft	Duffield	10	1.2	12
Yahoo	Yang	20	1.1	6
Amazon.com	Bezos	76	12	16
VC Late Ave				17
Bloomberg	Bloomberg	21	18	86
Dell	Dell	28	14	50
Nike	Knight	52	11	21
Abraxis BioScience	Soon-Shiong	2.9	2.9	100

Continental Rs	Hamm	11	5.6	51
Dish Network	Ergen	11	5.2	47
Menards	Menard	5.2	5.2	100
Schwab	Schwab	14	3.7	26
Gap	Fisher	10	2.3	23
No VC Ave				56

Wealth kept: Entrepreneur's net worth as of April 2012.

Wealth created: Venture's market capitalization—data for twenty-two entrepreneurs whose personal net worth is available from public sources.

About the Author

Dileep Rao was a venture financier. He led venture development and financing at one of the largest development finance institutions in the US where he managed five turnarounds, developed two incubators, financed businesses with equity, debt, leases, and development finance, and did private placements. He also consulted in new business development for entrepreneurs and Fortune 500 corporations.

Rao has interviewed and analyzed the strategies of America's best entrepreneurs to learn how they built their ventures. He writes about these strategies in his blog for Forbes.com and in his books. His last book with Inc. Magazine, *Nothing Ventured, Everything Gained: How Entrepreneurs Create, Control & Retain Wealth Without Venture Capital*, was an Amazon bestseller and shows how more than 9/10ths of America's billion-dollar entrepreneurs took off without VC by using skills and smart strategies. His free e-book, *The Truth About Venture Capital*, can help you select between skills and VC.

Rao has written other nationally acclaimed books including *Business Financing: 25 Keys to Raising Money* (NY Times Pocket MBA Series) and *Handbook of Business Finance & Capital Sources* (American Management Association).

Rao teaches unicorn-entrepreneurship and financing at Florida International University, Harvard, Stanford, INCAE, and the University of Minnesota. He also speaks and offers workshops on billion-dollar entrepreneurship and risk-reduced new venture development for entrepreneurs, innovators, and new business developers.

Rao has developed a unicorn-entrepreneurship program to help entrepreneurs, technologists, corporate new business developers, and students learn the skills to take off without VC. This program can also help banks, incubators, and governments to bridge the VC chasm from idea to Aha in their areas.

For the US government, Rao was a social entrepreneurship consultant and assisted fifteen community development corporations to develop ventures in low-income areas. He has also trained the top entrepreneurs in Haiti to grow more with less.

Dr. Rao has two engineering degrees and a doctorate in business administration from the University of Minnesota.

Endnotes

1   Dileep Rao, Bootstrap to Billions, 2009, www.dileeprao.com

2   (https://www.entrepreneur.com/article/332209).

3   http://archive.fortune.com/magazines/fortune/fortune_
    archive/1992/06/29/76578/index.htm

4   https://www.google.com/search?q=half+of+your+advertis-
    ing+is+wasted&oq=half+your+advertising+is+wasted&gs_l=psy-
    ab.1.0.0i22i30k1.14081.31843.0.33992.37.28.0.0.0.0.562.4537.2-
    5j4j2j2.13.0....0...1.1.64.psy-ab..27.9.2812...0j33i22i29i30k1.
    QWOBbfrCj68

5   Toni Mack, Communications: The Next Wave, Forbes.com,
    October 6, 1997

6   Steven Davidoff Solomon, New Share Class Gives Google
    Founders Tighter Control, *New York Times*, April 13, 2012, https://
    dealbook.nytimes.com/2012/04/13/new-share-class-gives-
    google-founders-tighter-control/

7   Erin Griffith, Mark Zuckerberg Controls Facebook and He
    Intends to Keep It That Way, Fortune.com, April 27, 2016, http://
    fortune.com/2016/04/27/zuckerberg-facebook-control/

8   Lucinda Shen, Meet the Snap IPO Billionaires, Fortune.com,
    March 3, 2017, http://fortune.com/2017/03/02/snap-ipo-
    snapchat-stock-evan-spiegel-net-worth/

9   Matthew Yglesias, All Hail, Emperor Zuckerberg, Slate.com,
    February 3,2012, http://www.slate.com/articles/business/
    moneybox/2012/02/facebook_s_ipo_how_mark_zuckerberg_
    plans_to_retain_dictatorial_control_his_company_.html

10 Sean Murphy, *Something Ventured: Make Money and Change the
    World for the Better*, October 10, 2016, https://www.skmurphy.com/

blog/2016/10/10/something-ventured-make-money-and-change-the-world-for-the-better/

11 Ali Montag, How Michael Dell turned $1,000 into billions, starting from his college dorm room, CNBC.com, February 26, 2018, https://www.cnbc.com/2018/02/26/how-michael-dell-turned-1000-into-billions-starting-from-his-dorm.html

12 Meet Amancio Ortega: The third richest man in the world, *Fortune*, January 8, 2013, http://fortune.com/2013/01/08/meet-amancio-ortega-the-third-richest-man-in-the-world/

13 Dileep Rao, Fastenal: Robert Kierlin, *Bootstrap to Billions*, 2009, www.dileeprao.com

14 Dileep Rao, Best Buy: Richard Schulze, *Bootstrap to Billions*, 2009, www.dileeprao.com

15 http://ask.metafilter.com/104341/From-where-did-this-Bill-Gates-quote-originate

16 *Handbook of Business Finance, 5th edition*, Dileep Rao, 2009 (dileeprao.com)

17 Marianne Hudson, Angel investment in the US—Trends and Best Practices, *Angel Capital Association*, September 26,2016, Angelcapitalassociation.org/data/Documents/ACAatAEBAN09-26-16.pdf

18 Theodore Schleifer and Rani Molla, Venture capitalists are spending more money on fewer deals, *Recode*, October 10, 2017, https://www.recode.net/2017/10/10/16448318/why-spend-invest-venture-capital-vc-deals-tech

19 https://paulcollege.unh.edu/research/center-venture-research/cvr-analysis-reports (2012 annual report)

20 Laura Huang, Why early-stage investors tend to trust their gut, *Knowledge@Wharton*, January 20, 2017, http://knowledge.wharton.upenn.edu/article/gut-feel-and-investing/

21 Ellen Rosen, Student's start-up draws attention and $13 million, *New York Times*, May 26, 2005, http://www.

nytimes.com/2005/05/26/business/26sbiz.html?_
r=3&scp=1&sq=thefacebook+parker&st=nyt&

22   Robert Wiltbank and Warren Boeker, *TechCrunch*.com, Returns to angel investors, November 2007, http://techcrunch. com/2012/10/13/angel-investors-make-2-5x-returns-overall/

23   http://www.angelcapitalassociation.org/press-center/angel-group-faq/

24   Erik Sherman, 5 things you must know about angel investors, Inc.com, (no date given), https://www.inc.com/erik-sherman/5-things-you-must-know-about-angel-investors.html

25   Andy Rachleff, Why angel investors don't make money...and advice for people who are going to become angels anyway, TechCrunch.com, September 30, 2012, https://techcrunch. com/2012/09/30/why-angel-investors-dont-make-money-and-advice-for-people-who-are-going-to-become-angels-anyway/

26   Marty Biancuzzo, What's your equity, *Wall Street Daily*, March 29, 2014, http://www.wallstreetdaily.com/2014/03/29/facebook-oculus-rift-crowdfunding/

27   Harry McCracken, Is crowdfunding the future of investments, *Fast Company*, https://www.magzter.com/article/Business/Fast-Company/Is-Crowdfunding-The-Future-Of-Investments

28   Mark Grandstaff, More turn to crowdfunding to help deal with unexpected debts, *USA Today*, March 9, 2017, http://www. usatoday.com/story/money/personalfinance/2017/03/09/more-turn-crowdfunding-help-deal-unexpected-debts/97258966/

29   Michael J. Miller, The rise of DOS: How Microsoft got the IBM PC OS contract, PCmag.com, August 10, 2011, http:// forwardthinking.pcmag.com/software/286148-the-rise-of-dos-how-microsoft-got-the-ibm-pc-os-contract

30   Michael J. de la Merced and Louise Story, Bloomberg expected to buy Merrill's stake in his firm, *New York Times*, July 17, 2008, http://www.nytimes.com/2008/07/17/business/17broker.html

31   https://www.sba.gov/sbic/general-information/program-overview

32   Emma Dunkley and Judith Evans, Retail investors at risk as big business enters P2P lending, *Financial Times*, May 25, 2015, https://www.ft.com/content/f294fd78-007a-11e5-a908-00144feabdc0

33   *Handbook of Business Finance, 5th edition*, Dileep Rao, 2009 (dileeprao.com).

34   Paul Gompers and Josh Lerner, The Venture Capital Cycle, *MIT Press*, 1999

35   Dileep Rao, Designing Successful Venture Capital Funds for Area Development, Applied Research in Economic Development, 2006 Volume 3, Number 2, pp. 27-37

36   Clayton Christensen, Disruptive Innovation, http://www.claytonchristensen.com/key-concepts/

37   Richard Harroch, A guide to venture capital financings for startups, Forbes.com, March 29, 2018, https://www.forbes.com/sites/allbusiness/2018/03/29/a-guide-to-venture-capital-financings-for-startups/#37f5e4951c9c

38   https://www.pwcmoneytree.com/MTPublic/ns/nav.jsp?page=historical

39   Paul Cohn, What is the average IRR achieved by venture capital funds, May 26, 2017, https://www.quora.com/What-is-the-average-IRR-achieved-by-venture-capital-funds

40   Dileep Rao, Fastenal: Robert Kierlin, Bootstrap to Billions, 2009, www.uentrepreneurs.com

41   Dileep Rao, Tastefully Simple: Jill Blashack Strahan, Bootstrap to Billions, 2009, www.uentrepreneurs.com

42   Honoring those we missed: The Anti-Portfolio, Bessemer Venture Partners, https://www.bvp.com/portfolio/anti-portfolio

43   Christine Lagorio-Chafkin, Kevin Systrom and Mike Krieger, Founders of Instagram, Inc., https://www.inc.

com/30under30/2011/profile-kevin-systrom-mike-krieger-founders-instagram.html

44 Bruce Upbin, Facebook buys Instagram for $1 billion. Smart Arbitrage. Forbes.com, April 9, 2012, http://www.forbes.com/sites/bruceupbin/2012/04/09/facebook-buys-instagram-for-1-billion-wheres-the-revenue/

45 https://en.wikipedia.org/wiki/Instagram

46 Statista: The Statistics Portal, https://www.statista.com/statistics/270290/number-of-ipos-in-the-us-since-1999/

47 How did Mark Cuban become rich, Yahoo.com, http://answers.yahoo.com/question/index?qid=1006042308537

48 Gary Rivlin, Segway's Breakdown, *Wired*, March 1, 2003, http://www.wired.com/wired/archive/11.03/segway_pr.html

49 Segway: Our story so far, Segway.com, http://www.segway.com/about-segway/segway-milestones.php

50 Gary Rivlin, Segway's Breakdown, *Wired*, March 1, 2003, http://www.wired.com/wired/archive/11.03/segway_pr.html

51 Michael Ewens and Matt Marx, "Research: What Happens to a Startup when Venture Capitalists Replace the Founder," *Harvard Business Review*, February 14, 2018

52 Pascal Levensohn, Rites of Passage: Managing CEO transition in venture-backed technology companies, Levensohn Venture Partners, 2006, http://www.levp.com/rites-of-passage-managing-ceo-transition-in-venture-backed-technology-companies/

53 Karl Ulrich's talk at the University of Minnesota, Developing New-Category Products, Allen D. Shocker Lecture, March 3, 2004, http://www.npdbd.umn.edu/useful-links/shocker-lecture/shocker-lecture-2004

54 Rollerblade Inc. History, Fundinguniverse.com, http://www.fundinguniverse.com/company-histories/rollerblade-inc-history/

55   The Rollerblade story: An entrepreneurial dream story, scottolson.com, http://scottolson.com/rollerbladestory.shtml

56   PWCMoneyTree.

57   eBoys: The first inside account of venture capitalists at work, Randall E. Stross, 2000

58   William A Sahlman, The structure and governance of venture-capital organizations. *Journal of Financial Economics*. 27, 473-521, 1990

59   Nicole Perlroth, How Andreessen Horowitz bunted on Instagram investment, *New York Times*, April 20, 2012, http://bits.blogs. nytimes.com/2012/04/20/how-andreessen-horowitz-fumbled-an-instagram-investment/?_r=0

60   Anderson, Howard, Good-Bye to Venture Capital, *MIT Technology Review*, June 2005

61   Steven N. Kaplan and Josh Lerner, It Aint Broke: The Past, Present, and Future of Venture Capital, *Journal of Applied Corporate Finance*, Volume 22, Number 2, A Morgan Stanley publication, Spring 2010

62   Adam Lashinsky, Kleiner Perkins gets its digital groove back on, *Fortune*, November 29, 2010, http://fortune.com/2010/11/29/kleiner-perkins-gets-its-digital-groove-back-on/

63   Cambridge Associates LLC, US Venture Capital Index and Selected Benchmark Statistics. June 30, 2010

64   Cambridge Associates quoted in "Good-Bye to Venture Capital" by Howard Anderson, *MIT Technology Review*, June 2005

65   Business Week, *Bloomberg*, July 4, 2005, p. 81

66   Andy Rachleff, Why angel investors don't make money, *TechCrunch*, September 30 2012, https://techcrunch.com/2012/09/30/why-angel-investors-dont-make-money-and-advice-for-people-who-are-going-to-become-angels-anyway/

67   Focus Ventures and Thomson Venture Economics, *Wall Street Journal* 5/27/04

68   Diane Mulcahy, Bill Weeks and Harold S. Bradley, We have met
      the enemy...and he is us, Ewing Marion Kauffman Foundation,
      2012, https://www.slideshare.net/kloeckner/kauffman-
      foundationventurecapital

69   http://www.cbinsights.com/blog/trends/silicon-valley-venture-
      capital-domination

70   Paul Gompers and Josh Lerner, The venture capital cycle, *MIT
      Press*, 1999

71   Small Business Investment Company Program. Financial
      Performance Report for Cohorts 1994–2004

72   Martin Kenney and Donald Patton, The Geography of
      Employment Growth: The Support Networks for Gazelle IPOs,
      SBA, May 2013

73   http://www.underarmour.jobs/our-history.asp

74   Finance.google.com (Data for underarmour)

75   Dileep Rao, *Bootstrap to Billions*, 2009, www.dileeprao.com

76   Dileep Rao, Best Buy: Richard Schulze, *Bootstrap to Billions*, 2009,
      www.dileeprao.com

77   Dileep Rao, UnitedHealth Group: Richard Burke, Bootstrap to
      Billions, 2009, www.dileeprao.com

78   Dileep Rao, Rapid Oil Change: Ed Flaherty, *Bootstrap to Billions*,
      2009, www.dileeprao.com

79   Nicholas Carlson, At last—the full story of how Facebook
      was founded, *Business Insider*, March 5, 2010, http://www.
      businessinsider.com/how-facebook-was-founded-2010-3?op=1

80   Ari Levy, Accel Facebook bet poised to become biggest venture
      profit: Tech, Bloomberg.com, January 17, 2012, http://www.
      bloomberg.com/news/2012-01-18/accel-s-facebook-bet-poised-
      to-become-biggest-ever-venture-profit-tech.html

81   Douglas MacMillan, How Mark Zuckerberg Hacked the Valley,
      Bloomberg BusinessWeek, May 21, 2012, page 62

of Saskatchewan, Value added by angel investors through post-investment involvement: Empirical evidence and ownership implications, Clevelandfed.org, March 10, 2009

83 Nicole Perlroth, How Andreessen Horowitz bunted on an Instagram investment, New York Times, April 20, 2012, https://bits.blogs.nytimes.com/2012/04/20/how-andreessen-horowitz-fumbled-an-instagram-investment/?_r=0

84 Dileep Rao, Finance Any Business Intelligently, IFC, 2008, www.dileeprao.com

85 Paul Gompers and Josh Lerner, The Venture Capital Cycle, MIT Press, 1999

86 PWCMoneyTree.com

87 Nicholas Carlson, Inside Groupon: The truth about the world's most controversial company, Business Insider, October 31, 2011, http://www.businessinsider.com/inside-groupon-the-truth-about-the-worlds-most-controversial-company-2011-10

88
     Fortune, April 18, 2005, p. 138

89 Jennifer Reingold, Southwest's Herb Kelleher: Still crazy after all these years, Fortune, January 14, 2013, page 97, http://fortune.com/2013/01/14/southwests-herb-kelleher-still-crazy-after-all-these-years/

90 Gerard Tellis (USC) and Peter Golder (NYC) in Regional Review, Fall 1996, Vol 6, No. 4, Federal Reserve Bank of Boston

91 10 bizarre and daring feats of salesmanship, Fortune: The art of selling, September 29, 2008, http://archive.fortune.com/galleries/2008/fortune/0809/gallery.Legends_of_sales_Clifford.fortune/index.html

92 Richard L. Brandt, Birth of a salesman, Wall Street Journal, October 15-16, 2011, page C2.

93   Charlie Rose, Charlie Rose talks to Roger Penske & team, Bloomberg BusinessWeek, May 30, 2011, page 24.

94   David A. Kaplan, Chipotle's growth machine, Fortune, September 26, 2011, page 135

95   Caleb Melby, Boardwalk Billionaire, Forbes, September 10, 2012, page 99

96   Michael Dell, How we got started, http://www.angelfire.com/extreme4success1/ch53.html

97   Dileep Rao, Spanlink: Brett Shockley, *Bootstrap to Billions*, 2009, www.dileeprao.com

98   Monte Burke, UnderArmour CEO Kevin Plank and his underdog horse farm, *ForbesLife*, September 2012, page 46, https://www.forbes.com/sites/monteburke/2012/09/07/under-armour-ceo-kevin-plank-and-his-underdog-horse-farm/#36885eae39de

99   Dinah Eng, John Paul DeJoria: Adventures of a serial entrepreneur, *Fortune*, April 30, 2012, page 23, http://archive.fortune.com/2012/04/24/smallbusiness/paul_mitchell_dejoria.fortune/index.htm

100   Dileep Rao, Tastefully Simple: Jill Blashack Strahan, *Bootstrap to Billions*, 2009, www.dileeprao.com

101   Dileep Rao, Medtronic: Earl Bakken, Bootstrap to Billions, 2009, www.dileeprao.com

102   Max Chafkin, Not just another web2.0 company, Yelp basks in its star power, FastCompany.com, December 2012/January 2013, page 126, https://www.fastcompany.com/3002950/not-just-another-web-20-company-yelp-basks-its-star-power

103   Dileep Rao, Conversation with Gustavo Cisneros at Florida International University (2012) and Gustavo Cisneros Pionner, Pablo Bachelet, Hispanic Publishing LLC, 2004.

104   Tony Hsieh, Redefining Zappos' business model, *Bloomberg BusinessWeek*, May 31, 2010, page 88, https://www.bloomberg.

com/news/articles/2010-05-27/tony-hsieh-redefining-zappos-business-model

105   Laura Berman, Making Detroit a tech hub—One mogul's vision, *Fortune*, November 23, 2009, page 76, http://archive.fortune.com/2009/11/10/news/companies/gilbert_detroit.fortune/index.htm

106   Lacey Rose, Shill shocked, Forbes, November 22, 2010, page 146, https://www.forbes.com/forbes/2010/1122/private-companies-10-guthy-renker-media-shill-shocked.html#15cf78ac170a

107   Karl Ulrich's talk at the University of Minnesota, Developing New-Category Products, Allen D. Shocker Lecture, March 3, 2004, http://www.npdbd.umn.edu/useful-links/shocker-lecture/shocker-lecture-2004

108   John Kenneth Galbraith, https://www.goodreads.com/quotes/476607-there-are-two-kinds-of-forecasters-those-who-don-t-know

Billions, Dileep Rao, 2009, www.dileeprao.com

Business Press

FIU Business Press equips professionals with the essential tools and skills for business success in a rapidly evolving world. An imprint of Mango Publishing, FIU Business Press is part of Florida International University's College of Business, a top-ranked school by *U.S. News & World Report*. The college has been recognized as the nation's #2 international business program, #8 international MBA, and #22 online master's in business. Based in Miami, FIU has been named a top-50 innovative public university and is the nation's fourth largest university with a student body of more than 54,000.

Mango Publishing, which publishes an eclectic list of books by diverse authors, was named 2019 and 2020's #1 fastest growing independent publisher by *Publishers Weekly*. Through a partnership of FIU College of Business office of Executive Education and Mango Publishing, FIU Business Press shares innovative, yet practical, business knowledge that allows professionals and executives to thrive globally.

Help us fuel business growth by sharing your thoughts and ideas:

Read about FIU's business programs:
business.fiu.edu/executive-education

Email us: FiuExecEd@fiu.edu

Follow us on LinkedIn:
Florida International University- College of Business
FIU Executive Education

Newsletter: mangopublishinggroup.com/newsletter